AF564985

INDIA FIRST

INDIA FIRST

K.R. Malkani

Ocean Books Pvt. Ltd.

ISO 9001:2015 Publishers

No part of this publication can be reproduced, stored in a retrieval system or transmitted in any form or by any means, electronic, mechanical, photocopying, recording or otherwise without the prior permission of the author and the publisher.

Published by
Ocean Books (P) Ltd.
4/19 Asaf Ali Road,
New Delhi-110 002 (INDIA)
e-mail: info@oceanbooks.in

ISBN 978-81-8430-630-9
INDIA FIRST
by Shri K.R. Malkani

Edition
2026

Price
₹600.00 (Rs. Six Hundred Only)

© Reserved

Printed at
Narula Printers, Delhi

Dedicated to
the Sacred Memory
of
Dr. Keshav Baliram Hedgewar
Founder of R.S.S.

FOREWORD

Shri Kewal Malkani has been an outstanding journalist. But, for him, journalism has not been just a profession; it has been a commitment to a cause. And this cause has been very aptly summed up in the title of this book, 'INDIA FIRST'.

I have known Malkaniji for over six decades now. When I entered college he was three years my senior and then he was appointed lecturer in that institution. Also, I have known him very closely. I have had my apprenticeship in journalism under him. As this compilation of articles would vividly bear out, more than a scribe, he is a thinker—and very bold and unorthodox one for sure. I am certain the present compilation of articles, ranging from 'The Soul of India' to 'Politicians and the Stars' will stimulate among the reading public, discussion and debate which will inspire more and more readers to accept the fundamental ideal that has motivated the author himself all his life, namely, *Rashtra Sarvopari*.

26.01.2002

—L.K. ADVANI

Preface

For quite some time many good friends of mine had been urging me to do a book on the major national issues of our time. But I soon realised that that is precisely what I have been doing all my writing life of more than half a century. Here is, therefore, a choice selection from the same, duly edited and updated and suitably supplemented with new writings—right up to the events of Sept. 11 and even Dec. 13, 2001.

We write in the Press. But the life of a daily paper is just one day. The life of a weekly is normally only one week. And how many readers will make cuttings of even the best writings—and maintain files?

Although journalism has been rightly described by Bernard Shaw as "literature in a hurry", some excellent stuff also gets published in the Press. However, it gets lost to posterity. Select compilations retrieve these nuggets of analyses and insights. For, a book is for ever.

A question may be asked about the title of the book: why INDIA FIRST? For the simple reason that issues here have been examined from the national, and not the so-called secular or socialist point of view. That is what RSS has taught me and countless others. And that is how men and matters have been viewed by me over the decades. Sound internationalism can be built only on the basis of healthy nationalism.

We in India have the tendency to run down our country, our people, our institutions. The conventional wisdom is that *Hindutva* is communal; that Manu was anti-woman and anti-Dalit; that India is over-populated; that Hindu-Muslim problem is insoluble; that globalisation is good; that computers are more important than History, et cetera, et cetera. For a change, here is an understanding and an appreciation of India, of Indians and of things Indian.

Manu was the greatest Law-giver of mankind; *Hindutva* is Indian nationalism; population is also power; employment is more important than GDP; with all our differences, Hindus and Muslims are blood brothers; globalisation is, for the most part, gobble-isation; history is the philosophy of nations; India is the beacon-light of the world.

It is not for nothing that India has survived the ravages of time and circumstance. India is unique. And INDIA FIRST is an effort at understanding why and how it is unique.

Francis Bacon has said: “Some books are to be tasted, others to be swallowed and some few to be chewed and digested.” The good reader is welcome to correspond—and even let the author know how much of INDIA FIRST was tasted, how much swallowed and how much digested.

B-51, New Rajendra Nagar
New Delhi-110060

—K.R. Malkani
Sankranti, 2002.

Contents

I. PHILOSOPHY

1. The Soul of India
2. Hindutva: What does it mean?
3. India was born Secular
4. History: The Philosophy of Nations
5. Is India a Soft State?

The Soul of India

'Eka Dharmarajya habe a Bharate'.
(Let there be one Dharma Rajya in Bharatvarsha.)

—*Rabindranath Tagore*

Religion has been the soul of India. As Swami Vivekanand put it: "In every nation you will have to work through their methods. To every man you have to speak in his own language. If you want to speak of politics in India, you must speak through the language of religion."

In pre-Muslim India, Hindu kings also fought wars. But the first thing the victorious king did was to go and worship the gods of the vanquished king. Gods were above and beyond kings. Even the Muslim rulers of India understood the centrality of religion in India. When the British offended the religious susceptibilities of Indians by greasing bullets with cow and pig tallow, they had the revolt of 1857 on their hands. Never again did they dare to tamper with the religion of Indians.

When the freedom movement started in India, it did so on a religious note. The appeal centred on *Desh* and *Dharma*. Bankim Chandra's *Vande Mataram* set the tone for the movement. And Rabindranath Tagore called for: *Eka dharmarajya habe a Bharate* (Let there be one Dharmarajya in Bharatvarsh).

A major reason why Mahatma Gandhi came to stand head and shoulders above other leaders was that he saw the centrality of religion in life. Declaring himself a 'staunch *Sanatani* Hindu', he said: "Politics divorced from religion was a corpse, fit only to be burnt." His whole idiom, from *Satya* and *Ahimsa* to *Brahmacharya* and *Aparigraha* was religious and moral.

The legitimisation of the religious content of nationalism continued for some time after Independence. The National Flag had the *Dharma Chakra* inserted in its centre. The Nehru cabinet decided to rebuild the Somnath mandir, desecrated and converted into a mosque by Mahmud Ghazni. But the general election in 1951-52 saw the entry of the term 'secularism' in the Indian political vocabulary for the first time.

The relevant philosophy here was *Sarva Dharma Sama Bhava*—equal respect for all creeds—ensuring justice for all. The importation of an alien concept has led to much misunderstanding. Hindus think that in 'secularism', Muslims have got something special, and they resent this 'appeasement'. Muslims find that 'secularism' is sound and fury, signifying nothing. They, therefore, feel cheated.

The Congress party is losing elections because it has lost much of both, Hindu and Muslim votes. And it has lost them both in a big way because it has abandoned the profound call of *Desh* and *Dharma*, which alone can move the masses, whether Hindu or Muslim, and opted for a placebo like secularism which is suspect in the eyes of both.

It is religion, says Toynbee, that "enables people to cope with the difficulty of being human, by giving spiritually satisfying answers to the fundamental questions about the mystery of the Universe and of man's role in it and by giving practical precepts for living in the Universe." The function of religion is "to ritualise man's optimism, to enhance his faith in the victory of hope over fear." Kingsley Davis in his *Human Society* writes: "Religion gives the individual a sense of identity with the distant past and the limitless future. It expands his ego by making his spirit significant for the universe and the universe significant for him."

It is only when the devout feel threatened that they become fundamentalist. Basically, 'fundamentalism' is a reaction against indiscriminate Westernisation and western support of autocratic regimes. In such a situation, the common Muslim can only invoke

the mosque as the instrument of mass mobilisation, and as the symbol of moral authority. It is only because society feels besieged in several Muslim countries—and besieged as it is by western military, economic and cultural domination—that it throws up fundamentalism as a defence mechanism. Islamic fundamentalists are basically anti-imperialist. When these foreign imperialist pressures cease, societies, now acting fundamentalist, will no doubt relax and become their natural, native, national selves.

Likewise, critics need to understand the nature of 'Hindu communalism' or 'fundamentalism'. Dr. Paulos Mar Gregorios, first metropolitan of the Delhi Diocese, says that the two schools of thought in the British government of India represented by Macaulay and Duff wanted Hinduism out. Macaulay's interest was to destroy Hinduism in order to overcome Indian resistance to colonialism. Alexander Duff's was to destroy Hinduism in order to plant Christianity in its place. The intention of both was to destroy Hinduism through English education. As a result 'the educated elite nurtured a major identity crisis in their souls for several generations.' This English education, writes Dr. Paulos, has 'culturally castrated' India. The key factor, he says, in restructuring the economy to make it strong, and restoring cultural vitality of the nation, can be nothing but the human factor and people's identity. Basically, the *Sangh Parivar* is a national striving in that direction.

United India having failed in 1947, and divided hostility having failed ever since, let us try peaceful and purposeful co-existence. Let Hindus in Pakistan not mind the Islamic appeal. And let Muslims in India not mind the Hindu appeal. That way we could have the best of both worlds, temporal and spiritual. We could live in peace as friendly neighbours; and we could also have our respective religious appeals.

(Note: A fuller elaboration of the above theme will be found in the author's contribution to 'Gandhi and the Changing Facets of India' published by Gandhi Smriti and Darshan Samiti, Rajghat, New Delhi-110002.)

□

Hindutva: What does it mean?

Politics bereft of religion are absolute dirt, ever to be shunned.

—Mahatma Gandhi

The secularists condemn the Sangh Parivar as communal, fascist and what not. But the Parivar has ceased to bother. The reason is simple: the Parivar sees itself as the continuation of the hallowed tradition of Dayanand and Vivekanand, Aurobindo and Tilak and, at a pinch, Gandhi. And the people of India confirm this by responding heartily to the call of *Hindutva* as the articulation of their innermost urges. As Ameury de Riencourt pointed out in his *Soul of India* 40 years ago: "Like every old civilisation still represented on this globe, India has been, and is increasingly, inspite of appearances, returning to its original sources. It is from the depths of that old civilisation that India is most likely to draw the strength needed to adapt itself to the modern world. Indian masses will only give their heartfelt allegiance to that party and ideology that appears to be a true emanation, more or less modernised no doubt, of some aspect or other of timeless Hinduism." It was, he noted, "Gandhism yesterday", and it can only be the "redoubtable RSS" tomorrow. And that is exactly how it is today.

Some well-known critics want a modernist definition of *Hindutva* that would be a true nationalist ideology acceptable to all the communities. This is a legitimate expectation. For most people are hearing the *mantra* of *Hindutva* for the first time—even as they heard the *mantra* of *Swadeshi* and *Swaraj* for the

first time in 1905. What exactly, they ask, *Hindutva* would mean?

Simply stated, *Hindutva* is Hindu-ness—'the character of being Hindu'. In the context of the partition of India, the concept of *Hindutva* no doubt has come to acquire a certain anti-Muslim connotation. But it does not have to be that. Basically, *Hindutva* is India's agenda for coming into its own after centuries of vicissitudes. Even Indian economy will come into its own and register a quantum jump—like the Pacific Tigers—only when the nation finds its feet, rediscovers its soul, takes pride in its past and has faith in its future.

But even more than that, India has to have such a cultural agenda because nations cannot live by GDP alone; they need to live by the spirit of their innermost being. That spirit in India is 'Hindu'. And Hindu is a culture, a whole national ethos, and not a creed or catechism.

People who want to separate religion from politics in the name of secularism, do not know what they are talking about. If a person seeks votes in the name of Ram or Rahim, he is obviously violating both, religion and politics. But if a person talks of *Ram Rajya*, he is only setting up idealistic goals, and he cannot be faulted. We don't have to divorce poetry from politics.

Also there are religions and religions. You could easily separate the Church from State in Europe because the Church and its chief, the Pope, had come from outside (from Rome or Constantinople) and this Church was trying to act as a super-state. But how exactly do you separate religion from politics in a country like India, where that religion is a native cultural growth, the very life-breath of the people?

Also, you cannot separate religion from politics when that religion is not organised in a central 'Church', and it is not interfering in the affairs of the state. In India, the role of religion in politics has traditionally been confined to a *Rajarishi*, who may only advise or warn on the moral issues involved in matters of state. Such a personage does not interfere in the affairs of the state. His presence would only give a moral tone to the state. That was why Gandhiji said, "Politics bereft of religion are absolute dirt,

ever to be shunned."

For another reason also, religion cannot be divorced from politics in India. A country's politics revolves around nationalism, and culture is an essential component of nationalism. In India, *Desh* and *Dharma* are two sides of the same coin. You never know where nationalism or national culture ends, and religion begins. No wonder the most popular patriotic Hindi song of the Freedom Movement in the thirties invited 'brave young men, to come and sacrifice yourselves in the cause of *Desh* and *Dharma.*'

As Wilhelm Von Pochhammer, German diplomat-historian, writes in his *India's Road to Nationhood*: "The Hindus' conception of God stems from their surroundings. Gods that have assumed human form or men that have been deified, like Rama and Krishna, are honoured as heroes and also as Gods. To the Hindus they are both heroes as well as Gods, and anyone who does not want to recognise Krishna as a God, has nevertheless to acknowledge him as a mythological hero.... This identity of religion with the nation has given Hinduism tremendous strength, toughness and length of life. It is these things that have enabled Hinduism to resist the onslaught of foreign religions, from ancient Vedic times down to the present day, and to keep a deep religiousness alive, as well as to revive it from time to time." No wonder Sri Aurobindo said: "The *Sanatan Dharma*, that is nationalism."

Such being the symbiotic relationship between *Desh* and *Dharma*, each reinforces the other, and you cannot separate the two. In the unlikely event of a divorce between *Desh* and *Dharma*, both would shrivel up and disintegrate.

However, this situation raises a question: How does Islam fit into a situation where nationalism has a Hindu base? The solution to this problem lies in understanding the separate role of religious belief and national culture. India has always recognised the absolute freedom of religion. Islam as a religion prescribes *Kalma* and *Haj, Roza* and *Namaz*, *Id* and *Zakat* etc., and Muslims have always had the fullest freedom to practise these. However, over the centuries, many Persio-Turco-Arabic customs, enforced by foreign rulers, have come to be considered as part of Islam. It

is these customs and practices that tend to raise a wall that divides Muslims from Hindus.

I am reminded of a small incident in the life of Sharat Chandra Chatterji, the well-known Bengali social novelist. He writes that once his servant had left him. When he turned up after a few months, Sharat first could not recognise him: his look, his manner, his dress, his idiom, all that had changed. He had become a 'Muslim'. The question is: Does an Indian have to become an imitation Arab or Iranian when he becomes a Muslim? Does he have to build a "Berlin Wall" around himself? This artificial wall needs to be removed.

For example, the Mughals used to celebrate not only the Idds and Nauroz, the Persian New Year day, but also Holi and Diwali, Vasant and Dussehra. Why should not the Indian Muslims celebrate these festivals? And why should they look upon invaders like Ghazni and Ghori—and not gems like Kabir and Dara—as heroes? They don't have to worship Rama and Krishna as gods; but why can't they adore them as heroes?

Persia was invaded and overwhelmed by Arabs. It went Muslim. But it has never excused the Arabs for defeating it thirteen hundred years ago in the battle of Qadesieh. Indeed, Iran went *Shiite* (literally, 'dissenter') to maintain its separate identity from Arabs, who were mostly *Sunni*. However, the Indian Muslim was made to follow an anti-Hindu line because that suited the Muslim Sultans ruling the mass of Hindus without their consent and against their will.

As a result, Islam in India very much grew as anti-Hinduism. I will here give just one example: the Prophet said that cow's milk is nectar and cow's flesh is poison. But in India conversion was linked to beef-eating, to snap the new Muslim's links with the old Hindu society and culture. The Indian Muslim is welcome to practise Islam; but he must cease to be anti-Hindu. Even Muslim Indonesia looks upon Rama as its greatest hero. Why even Iqbal wrote:

Hai Ram Ke Wujud Pe Hindustan Ko Naaz,
Ahl-e-Nazar Samajhte Hain Usse, Imam-i-Hind.

(India is proud of Ram; men of understanding see him as the

greatest national hero).

But the Indian Muslim is hesitant. The day Indian Muslims follow Iqbal and Indonesia, and cease to be anti-Hindu, there will be no Hindu-Muslim problem left. And that will solve the Indo-Pakistan problem too.

It will be asked: India has accepted many western influences; why does it not also accept Persio-Turco-Arabic influences that pass for 'Indian Muslim culture'? Why should it be allergic to them? Here the factual position is that over the centuries, many West Asian influences have been adapted and adopted. The *bagicha*, the *bazar*, the *surahi*, the *darzi*, the *gulab*, the *naan*, the *ghazal* and countless other things were found suitable; they were accepted and internalised. They became an integral part of Hindu or Indian culture. So it will be seen that the Hindu culture of today is *not* what it was a thousand years ago; like every other culture, it is already very much composite. But nobody can force things on it in the name of secularism, things it did not find suitable over the ages. The Indian Muslim should, therefore, relax, practise Islam and, for the rest, accept and enjoy Indian or Hindu culture as his very own. For truth to tell, all Indians are Hindu—by culture and nationality. France sees all Indians as 'Hindu' and Indian Hajis in Mecca have always been known as 'Hindi'.

Sir Syed Ahmed, founder of the Aligarh Muslim Education Movement, was once welcomed by the Hindu gentry of Gurdaspur, Punjab, as a 'great Muslim leader'. Sir Syed asked in surprise: "Am I also not Hindu?" Sir Syed was right. All Indians are Hindus—whether, by religious persuasion, we follow Siva or Vishnu, Buddha or Mahavira, Nanak, Jesus or Mohammed.

India cannot be rebuilt good and strong on the basis of a colourless and tasteless secularism; it will have to be revived on the basis of its own rich inclusive culture, what Sri Aurobindo calls 'the larger Hinduism'. That is what *Hindutva* is all about.

□

India was born Secular

Hindus will never stake their soul or body or property on religious controversy.

—Al-Biruni

HINDUS think Muslims are communal. Muslims think Hindus are communal. And Congressmen think they alone are secular. Fortunately all these impressions are wrong. Had it been otherwise, secularism would not stand the ghost of a chance in India. But the fact is that India has always been secular.

Indeed, throughout the freedom struggle, the word secularism was never a part of our political vocabulary. So much so that when the Constitution of India was framed and adopted, the word secularism did not occur in it even once. It was taken for granted as a fact of life. The term became current coin in India only after 1952 when our first General Elections were held. It is very much a child of our electoral politics.

Secularism as a modern concept was born in the West. There was a time when the Church ruled all Christandom. The Pope's writ ran in matters not only ecclesiastical but also temporal. Against this there was the revolt triggered by the Reformation.

The Christian princes heartily welcomed the new situation. They not only wanted freedom to marry or divorce as they pleased, but also the right to make war or peace, without any reference to the Pope. In the new redistribution of powers the Church was confined to religious affairs and the princes assumed sovereign authority in temporal matters. This separation of Church and State was described in one word as 'secularism'. Actually, before long Governments in many countries came to acquire a decisive voice even in religious matters.

The Indian tradition has been entirely different. Unlike the three Semitic religions (Judaism, Christianity and Islam) which have a fixed creed—for example, one God, one Prophet and one Holy Book—which must be believed in, Hinduism does not have any creed. It is a polytheistic congress of religious beliefs and practices. You may believe in one god or a million gods or no god, and yet be a Hindu. As Al-Biruni, the great historian who came to India with Mahmud Ghazni, noted: "At the most they (Hindus) fight with words, but they will never stake their soul or body or property on religious controversy." Hinduism has never been an organized Church with an hierarchy and a central authority.

Since anybody could have any religious beliefs, nobody was called upon to subscribe to any particular set of beliefs. The State did not prefer one or the other school of religious thought, although the monarch encouraged and enjoyed *Shastrarth*, great religious debates. The first thing a king who conquered new territory did, was to worship the gods of the annexed region.

Since Hinduism was a natural, and not a credal, religion, modern science did not rock its boat: if anything, it only seemed to confirm Hindu perceptions. And since there had been no break with the past, there was neither a Dark Age nor any renaissance. Politics and religion went their own independent ways. It was a state of perfect secularism. Interestingly enough, the only major case of departure from this norm was the Great Ashoka. He had a definite partiality for Buddhism. But his ministers effectively curbed his predilection by retiring him from the throne.

Even the Muslim rulers did not establish Islam as the State religion of India. Though many of them came from the rough steppes of Central Asia and gave India a harsh administration, they were basically political rulers and not religious zealots. One day when Alla-ud-din Khilji's attention was drawn to a Hindu religious procession passing below his palace, he expressed his inability to stop it. The much maligned Mohammed Tughlaq was accused by

Muslim historians of being an 'adorer of Hindus'. He met *yogis*, studied Sanskrit and took part in Holi festival. When on one occasion, the Chief *Qazi* named some Hindu leaders as conspiring against the Government, his reaction was: "This man desires the destruction of the empire. Cut off his head." And cut off it was!

The Mughals banned cow slaughter and drank only *Gangajal*. Indeed, basically, Mughals ruled India in coalition with Rajputs. Akbar's marriage with Jodhabai was a typical political-cum-matrimonial alliance. She not only retained her Hindu faith but very much Hinduized Akbar himself. Though Aurangzeb reversed this liberal tradition, he retained Jaipur and Jodhpur as the pillars of the State. He did not touch Shivaji in captivity for fear of displeasing Jaipur. And he trusted only Hindus to guard his private apartments.

Shivaji rose in revolt against the bigotry of Aurangzeb; but he never offended Muslim religious susceptibilities. He killed Afzal Khan for political reasons—but he built him an impressive tomb on the spot for courteous reasons. He never desecrated a mosque. And although he married as many as seven times—mostly for political reasons—he was too conscientious to accept the captive daughter of the *subedar* of Kalyan.

The British followed the Indian tradition. In the affairs of the East India Company, trade was paramount and the missionaries ploughed a lonely furrow. When British rule was firmly established, there were some attempts at proselytization. But 1857 convinced them of the futility of an active religious policy. From then on, they bent over backwards to respect the religious feelings of all sections of the population.

In 1921 we made the mistake of mixing up religion with politics when India's freedom movement was linked to the demand for the restoration of the Khalifa of Islam. (Be it said to the credit of Jinnah that he opposed that programme.) The partition of India can be directly traced to the religious passions a roused by that issue. But otherwise it was a very secular movement, based on *Swadeshi*, taking up issues like *khadi* and salt tax laws, the exchange rate and Indianisation of the services.

When India became free, we gave ourselves a Constitution that gave equality of status to all its citizens without any differences of caste, class or creed. It is significant that though the wounds of partition were still fresh, nobody suggested anything less than full citizenship rights for Muslims. Nobody so much as whispered that Muslims could not be entrusted with crucial offices like those of President, Prime Minister and Army Chief of Staff.

Indian secularism was not a favour done to Muslims or to anybody else. It was only a modern expression of the age-old Indian tradition that all religious paths are equally valid, that the State has no religion and that nobody may be discriminated against on grounds of religious belief.

Some Muslims have the feeling that the Indian State has a Hindu character and that, to that extent, it is not quite a secular State. For example they do not relish All India Radio beginning the day's programme with *bhajans*. They do not fancy *bhoomi-pujans* and chanting of hymns at foundation-laying ceremonies. When we launch a ship by breaking a coconut—and not by breaking open a bottle of champagne, as is the British custom—they think Hindus are being religious and not secular. Some of them even object to the statues of Yaksha and Yakshi outside the Reserve Bank Building in New Delhi's Parliament Street.

Such objections are based on misunderstanding. India is a democratic country. And this democracy is overwhelmingly Hindu. It is, therefore, inevitable that the Hindu life-style should manifest itself in all aspects of Indian life. This is not communalism at work: it is, rather, a case of a working democracy.

A people's culture is part of their life. Secularism does not mean that they have to strip themselves of their culture when dealing with public affairs, like the snake which sheds its skin with the seasons. A people's culture lends colour and flavour and music to all its activities. It is to be understood and appreciated, and not excluded in the name of a colourless, tasteless and odourless concept of secularism. Whenever the British government orders fresh elections, the Prime Minister, the leader of the Opposition and other

political leaders jointly attend Church of England services in Westminster Abbey. This is part of Britain's national tradition. British Catholics and Jews do not view it as Anglican communalism.

Muslim Indians should also accept the *Kalash* and the coconut; the conchshell and the *kum kum* as part of our colourful national heritage. Rafi Ahmed Kidwai understood this situation very well when he urged Nehru to ban cow slaughter, since 'that is what the people want'. He went on to say in good humour that if he became PM he would do such popular things that people would forget all about Nehru. Dr. Zakir Hussain was also only respecting national tradition when, on his election as President of India, he called on the Shankaracharya of Shringeri Math to pay his respects. Mahatma Gandhi was not being communal when he talked of *Satya* and *Ahimsa*, he was only invoking the national ethos.

Some new-style secularists were surprised that Nehru was given a Vedic funeral. They forgot that Nehru had gone through all the religious ceremonies appropriate to a man of his caste and class. He was not only 'Pandit' to everybody from Cabinet colleagues down to butlers, he hardly ever missed a Kumbh Mela in his life. It was Nehru who insisted on putting the *Dharma Chakra* in the national flag. When Feroze Gandhi, a Parsi by birth, married his daughter, Nehru had the marriage solemnized according to Vedic rites. Feroze was also given a Hindu funeral. It is true that Nehru described himself a 'pagan'; but so is every Hindu!

In doing all this, Gandhi and Nehru were not being communal; they were only being natural, national. They knew there was no contradiction in being Hindu and secular. As Balasaheb Deoras of the RSS puts it "India is secular only because it is Hindu".

□

Huntington on Hindu Secularism

Only in Hindu civilization were religion and politics so distinctly separated. In Islam, God is Caesar; in China and Japan, Caesar is God; in Orthodox Russia, God is Caesar's junior partner.

—*Samuel Huntington*
'The Clash of Civilizations' (p. 70)

History: The Philosophy of Nations

May my son study History, for it is the only true philosophy of nations.

—*Napoleon*

Of late there has been much comment on certain changes in school text-books in U.P. Although much of the comment has been critical, there has also been a significant measure of appreciation. The end-result is a lively debate.

It will be readily conceded that school texts—particularly the history books—are important. They basically help form the national mind. The Britishers had prepared history texts with imperial interest in mind. For example, until a hundred years ago, Vikramaditya was a household name in India and Ashoka was practically unknown. But history books left out Vikramaditya completely and praised Ashoka to the skies. The reason was obvious: Vikramaditya had driven out the foreign invaders Shaka or Scythians, and Ashoka had gone non-violent. A non-violent Indian ruler suited the British rulers better than an Indian king who had driven out foreigners. Lord Curzon had candidly described all this selective and speculative history as 'the furniture of empire'. And it is sad to note that even after independence, we continued the old pattern of history, with only the role of Congress and some Congress leaders thrown in.

This was doing scant justice to Indian history and to the Indian mind. In the history of the freedom movement, they could not possibly leave out Mahatma Gandhi; but, for the rest, the focus

was mostly on one particular family. It tended to neglect the great trinity of Lal-Bal-Pal. It had no use for either the great liberals or the great revolutionaries. And there was a special allergy to Netaji Subhas Chandra Bose. The U.P. Government, therefore, has done well to try correct these imbalances.

U.P. has also included a lesson on Dr. Hedgewar, the man who founded the RSS. Dr. Hedgewar was one of those gems of the purest ray serene who shunned all publicity. But the national mind would be poorer for not knowing the well-springs of RSS-BJP-VHP inspiration which has spread all over the land, and even abroad.

Nor will it do to feed the national mind on an uncritical acceptance of all that the Congress ever did. For example, some school books praise the *Khilafat* movement as a great churner that united Hindus and Muslims. But fact of the matter is that this churning movement produced more poison than *Amrit.* It overnight converted *mullahs* into Muslim political leaders and ended up in large-scale Hindu-Muslim violence. No wonder many came to see it as *Akhil Aafat*, total disaster. Indeed the *Khilafat* movement sowed the seeds of partition. Any lesson on *Khilafat* movement must record both its credit and debit side, and note that it did more harm than good.

Nor need anybody be surprised by the importance that the RSS Parivar and the people of India give to Shivaji, Rana Pratap and Guru Govind Singh. They represented the will of the people, as against the state power of the rulers. For the same reason we give more importance to the leaders of the Freedom Movement than to the Viceroys.

With a view to dividing the people, the British floated many theories. The theory of Aryan invasion was invented to divide the South from the North. Although Hindus and Muslims had jointly fought the British in 1857, the history of the 'Muslim' period was written in a manner to divide the two societies. Until then, the Central Asian invaders were known in India as 'Turushk' or Turk. The British renamed their rule as 'Muslim' period and so forged an empathy between foreign invaders and local Muslims. (By the

same token, British rule should have been designated as 'Christian Period'!)

They further ensured this division by alternately favouring the one or the other—and by conferring on the Muslims, separate electorates, reservations and weightages.

They divided the Hindus and Sikhs of the Punjab by getting their stooge, Sardar Kahan Singh, a minister of Nabha, to write the thesis in 1899 that *Hum Hindu Nahin Hain* (We are not Hindus). Even the Maharaja was shocked to read this and he wondered aloud: 'If Sikhs are not Hindus, how shall we inter-marry?' He even got another Sardar to pen the pamphlet: *Hum Hindu Hain* (We Are Hindus). But the mischief had been done; a separatist school of thought had been brought into being.

School histories have done nothing to right these textual wrongs. For example our children continue to be taught that 'Aryans invaded India'. Now it is true enough that people have been moving around all through history. People have been coming into India; people have also been going out of India. But there is no proof of any kind—literary, architectural or any other, not even a folklore tradition—of any 'Aryan invasion' that over-turned the country and gave it a wholly new orientation. The Indus Valley Civilisation is said to be pre-Aryan; but it is as Indian as anything. The word 'Arya' has been used for 'a noble one', and not for 'a race', noble or otherwise. When Sita addressed Rama as "Hey Arya" obviously she did not belong to a race different from that of Rama. Indeed experts are of the opinion that 'Arya' is not the name of a race; it is only a linguistic group. It was the 19th century racists of Europe who launched the race theory to place themselves above the Black, Brown and Yellow peoples—and of course above the Jewish people. But our school texts blindly teach 'Aryan invasion of India' and so poison Indian society by providing a 'rationale' for Dravida Kazhagam.

These same texts tell our children the British version that Alexander defeated Porus and conquered and annexed the north-western areas of the country. The British object in exaggerating Alexander's performance in India was clear; they wanted to impress

upon our people that we had always been ruled by invaders—whether those invaders were 'Aryans', Alexander or Turks. All this was done to rationalise and justify British rule in India. But we unthinkingly repeat the British imperial propaganda in our books. Fact is that no Indian record mentions Alexander; obviously they viewed him as one of those border raiders. But even Greek records leave one in no doubt that he had a very bad time in India. After the Porus-Alexander battle, Porus had more territory than before. Alexander's troops were too terrified to proceed towards Patliputra (Patna), the capital of the Mauryas. Even king Sabbas of Sindh made his life miserable and the Greek historians noted: "They pierced his ribs with a spear... they gave him a weighty club blow on the neck...word went round in the Greek camp that Alexander was dead. Alexander had known his first defeat...."

Alexander had entered India with 1,20,000 foot soldiers and 15,000 cavalry; he left India with only a quarter of that force. As Marshal Zhukov, the greatest Russian General of World War II, pointed out, Alexander had been defeated in India. But our school texts continue to echo the British propaganda line that 'world-conquering' Alexander had succeeded in India!

Some people think India rejected Buddhism. They do not know that India absorbed Buddhism. Today, India's Hindu is more Buddhist than the Buddhist of Burma or Sri Lanka.

All medieval history tells you that Hindus invariably lost at Muslim hands. If that, indeed, was so, how is it that India survived as a predominantly Hindu country? The real victory in the 800-year-old war went to the Hindus, and not to the Muslims. Muslims won battles; Hindus won the war.

Some people say Hindus have no sense of history. What then are the *Itihasas* and *Puranas*? In any case, the Hindu has to deal with so much time and space, that no list of kings or conquerors will do justice to the subject. He, therefore, does not deal only with time; he also deals with the timeless. The myths are the simplified quintessense of history, philosophy and wisdom in immortal verse, over countless ages. People who dismiss the *Ramayana*, the *Mahabharat* and the *Bhagwat Purana* as 'myths', do not know

what they are talking about. The historic plays of Shakespeare have done more to mould British character and British institutions than all the court records and so-called 'histories' of early British royalty. In the words of good old Aristotle, 'Fiction is truer and more philosophical than history.' There is more historic truth in 'myths' than in so-called history books. As Arnold Toynbee notes in his *A Study of History*:

"History, like the drama and the novel, grew out of mythology, a primitive form of apprehension and expression in which —as in fairy tales listened to by children, or in dreams dreamt by sophisticated adults—the line between fact and fiction is left undrawn. It has, for example, been said of the *Iliad* that anyone who starts reading it as history will find that it is full of fiction but, equally, anyone who starts reading it as fiction, will find that it is full of history. All histories resemble the *Iliad* to this extent, that they cannot entirely dispense with the fictional element. The mere selection, arrangement and presentation of facts is a technique belonging to the field of fiction, and popular opinion is right in its insistence that no historian can be 'great' if he is not also a great artist." Valmiki and Vyas were great artists.

Some friends have made fun of 'Hindu Science' and 'Vedic mathematics'. But fact of the matter is that ancient India had made much progress in these fields. The steel pillar near Qutab Minar, Delhi, is proof of Indian advances in Chemistry. The concept of 'zero' was developed in India. Indian textiles were the rage of Europe until the early 19th century—when the hands of the muslin-weavers of Dhaka were cut off and high tariff walls raised to protect the British textile industry. Surgery was highly developed in India until Buddhism frowned on the dissection of bodies. Our *Ayurveda* and *Siddha* systems of health and longevity are relevant even today. England's bigger and best ships until the Napoleonic wars were being built in India. Long before Pythagoras, the theorem now known by his name had been worked out by Bodhayana. Indeed all these and many more facts of ancient Indian scientific advance are mentioned in the Government of India's own Science Exhibition on Pragati Maidan, Delhi. The only crime of the U.P.

Government is that it has taken things out of the museum and put them in the classroom.

The general misconception is that we have always been an other-worldly people, doing *Yoga* and *Homa* and, for the rest, wallowing in ignorance and superstition. What is wrong with making people aware of our great achievements in science and in the arts of life?

These are not small things. They have great significance. They establish our national identity and clarify our future course. Some State Governments have done well to go to the root of the matter in respect of motivation for national reconstruction. Dozens of German principalities uniting to form the German nation-state, was the doing of German history professors. Napoleon's only worry on his death-bed was: "May my son study history, for it is the only true philosophy of nations." Why, today even USA is revising its history books, bringing Columbus down a few notches. For, it is pointed out, was he not the man who brought intolerance and violence to the Americas? In launching the revision of history books, Lucknow and Bhopal have only followed the world trend towards correcting old unhappy imperial imbalances.

□

The whole World needs India

India which the whole world needs, and which alone needs no one.

—Voltaire

May the genius of India marry the genius of the world. India is the only great civilization not devoured by the West.

—Romain Rolland

The fascination and the sacredness of India have grown upon me.

—Lord Curzon

Is India a Soft State?

It is amazing how a country invaded so many times could maintain its identity.

—Karl Marx

Is India a soft State? Yes—and no.

From one point of view no State is all that soft. Every State has its police and military. And no State is all that hard. Beyond a point, even a dictatorship has to take note of domestic and foreign public opinion. However, it would be true enough to say that in a given situation some States will act softer than some others. It is a matter of their history, culture and vital national interests.

On many occasions we in India act soft. There are too many infractions of the law—and too few convictions. Not only ISI but even CIA and FBI play many games with us—for example the blowing up of Air India's 'Kanishka' and the mysterious air-dropping of lethal weaponry in Purulia—and get away with the same. Perhaps no other State in the world would have returned Ninety thousand plus Prisoners of War to Pakistan without getting it to sign the final solution of the Kashmir issue on the dotted line. (Good old Haksar thought—I think wrongly—that would have been like imposing a vindictive Versailles Treaty on Pakistan.) All this is true enough. But we do not need to be a hard, harsh State, so as not to repeat such lapses. We only need to be, and to act, a strong State. However, there are reasons enough for our not acting tough.

Old societies, rich in race experience, tend to act cool. They are not easily excited. As the poet put it, throughout the middle

ages, the Indian people "let the legions thunder past, in patient, deep disdain". Even earlier on, India declared *Ahimsa Paramo Dharmah* (non-violence is the highest religion). There are people in India who would not kill even a snake. And some of them view even milk-drinking as an inhuman infringement of the rights of cows and calves. No wonder men like Buddha and Mahavira could be born only in India and not anywhere else.

Gandhiji did not begin his public life with *Ahimsa*. When he returned from South Africa during World War I, he actually addressed Recruitment Melas, to persuade people to join the war effort. But he soon realised that an appeal to war and violence did not much appeal to the Indian people. And so he promptly and wisely switched over to non-violence.

In modern times this ancient thinking has been reinforced by our present situation. India is a huge and pluralist country with an infinite variety and complexity of castes, creeds and regions. It is like a convoy, which has to move slowly to carry all—or most—sections of the population.

This slow and deliberate movement is further necessitated by our democratic institutions. China liquidated fifty lac "reactionaries" in 1949—and another two crores in the 'Great Leap Forward'. In India even one killing makes the front page and disturbs the people. And that is probably as it should be—in a civil society.

There is yet another factor making for the comparative softness of the Indian State. Modern Indian has had little experience in the exercise of sovereignty. After Prithviraj Chauhan a thousand years ago, Indian sovereignty went into 'Turkish' hands. This was partly recovered by Vijayanagar, Sikhs and Marathas, but after 1761, it went straight into British hands. As Clive rightly remarked at that time: "Sovereignty had fallen to the ground, for anybody to pick it up." The East India Company picked it up—and handed it over to London. It was this inexperience in the exercise of sovereignty—involving issues of War and Peace—that caused Mrs. Indira Gandhi and her Kashmiri caucus to bungle the Shimla negotiations in 1972.

However, notwithstanding these factors making for softness,

India has not done too badly—too softly—since Independence. Many in the West expected India to disintegrate after 1947. We have only integrated the country more strongly—and that too democratically—since. We did cut a very sorry figure in 1962; and only the Gen. Henderson Brookes and Gen. P.S. Bhagat report on the India-China War can tell, why. (It is to be hoped that the Government makes that long-suppressed Report public in the interest of truth and transparency.) When, however, Pakistan acted funny in 1965, we gave them a bloody nose. Some Americans had thought that their Patton tanks would help Pakistan reach Delhi, and that India would soon be shifting its Capital to Hyderabad or Bangalore. In the event, however, it was the Indian Army thrust that caused Lahore Radio Station to air mourning music (*Marsiya*). And our gentle Prime Minister, Shri Lal Bahadur Shastri, actually cut a Patton Tank Cake on his next birthday and said he had felt like taking a walk in Lahore.

India not only dared to go nuclear, we confidently faced Western sanctions. And the Governor of the Bank of England himself came down to attend a Yashwant Sinha meeting in London, to understand how India was able to handle the sanctions with aplomb. And when Pakistan again played games—this time in Kargil—we again gave them a bloody nose. Soon after, when its sophisticated naval surveillance plane 'Atlantique' violated Indian air space we coolly shot it down. These are not the responses of a 'soft' State.

More recently their agents hijacked our plane. We released three terrorists to save the lives of 155 passengers and crew. But we don't have to be ashamed of it. (Even a steely State like Israel released as many as 31 terrorists in 1985 to save the lives of 153 passengers of a TWA plane.) And at the end of it all, we have put Pakistan squarely in the dock by establishing the Pakistani nationality of the hijackers. Even the US State Department spokesman blamed Pakistan with the statement that "there are agencies of the Government of Pakistan which have provided general support to a number of groups active in Kashmir, and that includes the Harkat."

It will thus be seen that India can be cool and gentle as a

cow. But this cow has horns which it can use to gore the enemy—if, as and when necessary. Our basic nature is as benign as Durga. But we can also switch over to Kali.

The difference between a 'soft' India and a 'hard' Pakistan is exemplified by the treatment we meted out to two erring leaders. Pakistan toppled, and then hanged Bhutto for rigging the election in a few constituencies. But, for the sin of declaring Emergency, India was content to just throw Mrs. Gandhi out of office. And when Home Minister Charan Singh got her arrested, public sympathy quickly turned in her favour. The Indian response was at once more mature and more democratic. The typical Indian response to a crisis, is: *Koi Baat Nahein* (it does not matter), *Sab Theek Ho Jayega* (It will all end well). While global winds blow around us, our response is *Phir Bhi Dil Hai Hindustani*. (We are Indians at heart—and our heart is in the right place).

USA has long been a hard and violent society. European settlers in North America liquidated men (Red Indians), animals and primeval forests with criminal abandon. When, therefore, President Kennedy was shot dead, a significant comment was that "violence is as American as apple-pie." In the American Civil War in the 19th century, more than a million people were killed. (The partition of India was a terrible thing. But even so, the number of killed did not exceed even one lac in the Punjab).

USA cynically dropped nuclear bombs on Japan in 1945, even though the latter had already offered to surrender. When, however, a few years later, Gen. MacArthur wanted to atom-bomb Korea, to the horror of British Premier Attlee—President Truman promptly dismissed him. So USA also can be less than hard.

When Iran seized the American Embassy, took its staff as hostages and kept them captive for 444 long days, USA did not dare to attack Iran. And even its attempt to free the hostages through commando action failed miserably. Not only that, Republican Party leaders, including Reagan and Kissinger, privately advised Iran *not* to release the hostages, since that would put a big feather in the cap of Democratic President Carter—and ensure his re-election! They wanted Reagan elected.

In the early sixties, USSR had installed some nuclear missiles in Cuba to threaten USA. Under Kennedy's strong protest, Khrushchov had to withdraw the same. But as *quid pro quo*, USA also had to remove its nuclear missiles in Turkey, which were a threat to USSR. It is a different matter that US control of much of the world media succeeded in very much suppressing the Turkish part of the news.

The position is that today even USA, very fortunately, does not have the stomach for war. The arrival of "body bags" from Somalia shown on TV was more than Americans could stand. It quickly withdrew from the scene. Today USA is supplying wheat to nuclear North Korea, so that it does not go berserk!

While thinking of soft States and hard States, one great historical example inevitably comes to mind—the example of ancient Greece. That civilization gave rise to two great antithetical city-States—Athens and Sparta. Athens was 'soft', Sparta was 'hard'. Sparta brought up its boys mostly as soldiers. Athens had its soldiers no doubt, but more than that it had its poets and parliamentarians, artists and philosophers. To this day the world remembers Socrates and Plato, Homer and Pericles of Athens. Who remembers anything or anybody from Sparta?

Perhaps India has been wise to be soft when it may, and hard only when it must. It returned Haji Pir Pass to Pakistan in 1966 to ensure the sanctity of ceasefire line. And it used the same logic of ceasefire line in Kargil in 1999, to pit the world against Pakistan. As Karl Marx noted in *Das Kapital*: "It is amazing how a country invaded so many times in its long history and under the control of an alien ruler for hundreds of years, could maintain its identity. It is all because of the richness of its culture which is rooted in villages that did not change with the change in rulers and dictators." And Max Muller, the translator of the *Vedas*, marvelled: "The more I try to unravel the mystery of India, the deeper it becomes. So amazing is the country, so wonderful its people and their culture."

Similar was the reaction of distinguished foreigners on the hijacked IC-814, Dec. 2000. Shirley Macklin, a Canadian lady, told the Winnipeg Free Press Journal in the Canadian High Com-

mission in New Delhi: “Since I’ve been off the plane, my feeling is that Indian people, what I know of them, are so sweet and loving to one another I don’t think they can believe that anyone can actually be that evil.”

And Roberto Giori, who owns the Lausanne-based Company De La Rue Giori, which controls ninety per cent of the world’s currency printing business, told *Time* (Jan. 17): “What I experienced on the plane has changed me forever. I don’t know what it is: Hinduism, the so-called fatalism of Indians. But the way the passengers stayed so calm throughout, even the children, was exemplary. I told myself, if the plane had been full of Italians or French, it would have been very different.”

“Blessed”, said Jesus, “are the meek; for they shall inherit the earth.” To be meek is not necessarily to be weak.

□

‘India does not belong to you, Mr. Nehru!’

Charles de Gaulle told me: "Tell Nehru not what we can give India but what India can give us. It is not the Indian who makes India. It is India that makes the Indian.........

Europe is suicidal, destructive. It is a cemetery of ideas. You mock at death with fire. We face death with cemetery......... And what is India? India is Ajanta. Picasso might have to live another life for his supreme vision of Shiva........."

—Andre Malraux
French Philosopher-Statesman &
de Gaulle’s first Ambassador to
Independent India.
(Raja Rao: The Meaning of India)

II. POLITY

1. Improving the Constitution
2. The Politics of Reservation
3. Solving the Kashmir Problem
4. The Bangla Flood
5. Prime Ministers vs Presidents
6. Case for National Government

Improving the Constitution

Seats should be reserved for women in the Rajya Sabha.

Recently the Government of India appointed the 'National Commission to Review the Working of the Constitution' and 'examine in the light of the experience of the past 50 years, as to how best the Constitution can respond to the changing needs of efficient, smooth and effective system of governance and socio-economic development of modern India within the framework of Parliamentary democracy, and to recommend changes, if any, that are required in the provisions of the Constitution, without interfering with its basic structure or features.'

Considering the fact that the BJP and its allies—the National Democratic Alliance—had made this a part of their Election Manifesto, Government was fully justified in appointing this Commission. And Congress criticism of the move as tampering with the Constitution sounds hollow. When in power, the party had amended the Constitution on an average of twice a year. Not only that, during the Emergency, 1975-77, it thought of subverting the Constitution altogether. There was a proposal to cancel elections, call a new Constituent Assembly and meanwhile make Mrs. Gandhi President of India for life! The then three Congress Governments of Punjab, Haryana and U.P. even adopted resolutions to this effect (*vide* P.N. Dhar's 'Indira Gandhi, Emergency and Indian Democracy').

However in view of the fact that Government does not have

even a simple majority in one of the two Houses of Parliament, it is not clear how it will muster a two-thirds majority to carry any amendments to the Constitution—unless it is assured of Congress support. This support has been forthcoming on 'economic reform' because the West and its MNCs are interested in it; but it is unlikely to be available for Constitutional reform, in which they have no particular interest. The whole exercise may, therefore, end up in nothing much. But at the same time it could highlight major Constitutional issues and heighten public awareness of the same. And that would be no mean achievement.

There are three amendments that are crucial to the health, strength and good conscience of our Democratic Republic. These pertain to the stability of the Government, a statutory ceiling on the number of ministers, and the need to require ratification of all international agreements.

The way the then Vajpayee Government was voted out by one frivolous vote in April 1999, left a very bad taste in the mouth. The old government was dead but a new one was powerless to be born. Such silly situations must be ended for good by requiring, as under German Law, that the Opposition must show majority support for its candidate for Prime Ministership, before it can be allowed to move a vote of non-confidence in the incumbent.

A second issue that needs immediate tackling is the size of ministries. Since there is no ceiling on the number of ministers, there are cases of mini-states with just forty MLAs, having thirty-six ministers. U.P. has almost hundred ministers and Bihar is not far behind. A Parliamentary Committee had recommended an upper limit of 10% in the case of a Unicameral House—and 11% in the case of a bicameral legislature. Some such rule needs to be enacted into law to prevent jumbo cabinets from making a mockery of our democracy.

A third issue is the ratification of all international agreements. In the absence of such a provision, Government has been entering into agreements extremely unpopular in the country. A classic example is World Trade Organisation. MNCs can browbeat a Government; but they cannot browbeat an entire Parliament. USA used

this ratification clause in its Constitution to reject Versailles Treaty and add conditionalities to WTO treaty. We should do the same. It will be a valuable instrument in the hands of a conscientious Government to protect its national interest. There are some other issues also that deserve positive consideration.

- Article 30 of the Constitution recognises the right of religious and linguistic minorities to establish and administer educational institutions of their choice. So while Muslims and Christians can do it, Hindus can't. There is no reason why Hindu religious organisations and denominations also should not have the right to run their own schools—even as Muslims and Christians do. We also need to consider whether children should not have the fundamental right to receive moral instruction through their own religious teaching.

When a SC man changes his religion, he loses his reservations and other special rights. But when a ST man changes faith, he retains all his special rights. This contradiction needs to be corrected. ST converts to, say, Christianity, not only enjoy all the old rights, they get all the foreign finance for education and employment. As a result, Christian tribals, though a small minority, corner the lion's share of ST reservations in the services.

We may also consider open voting—in place of secret ballot—for the election of Vidhan Parishad and Rajya Sabha members—to get round the Money Power in these elections.

Some countries provide for dual citizenship of their citizens. They can retain their original citizenship even when they acquire a new one. We should give the same facility to Indians abroad.

Of late there has been much debate about women's empowerment. Instead of reserving constituencies for them, we should reserve a certain number of seats for them in all the Upper Houses. This will bring many talented women to the legislature without subjecting them to the rough and tumble of a general election.

The appointment of a Constitutional Review Commission amounts to a churning of the Constitutional law and practice. One can only hope the end-result will be more *Amrit* and no poison.

□

The Politics of Reservation

The problem is not reservations but KHAM & AJGAR, MAJGAR & M-Y.

A few years back the country was been rocked by anti-reservation agitations. Educational institutions were closed, buses burnt, trains stopped in their tracks. The Police responded with firing which resulted in many deaths.

Although the occasion was the decennial extension of reservation of Assembly and Parliament seats for Scheduled Castes and Scheduled Tribes, the agitation was not directed against that but against reservation of seats in professional institutions and for jobs at the Centre and in the States. And the two issues got mixed up only because the PM assured 'reservations'—seeming to imply *all* of the above—and because of his party's commitment to implement the Mandal Report, extending reservations in admissions and recruitment to Other Backward Classes that is other than SC and ST.

On the Vidhan Sabha and Lok Sabha seats reservation issues, it is the SC who would have a grievance. The original arrangement was that areas that were to return SC candidates were constituted into two-member constituencies. All voters in this area had two votes. The candidate, *Savarna* or *Avarna*, who polled maximum votes, was declared elected and from among *Avarna* candidates, the one who polled the most votes was declared elected. This arrangement worked very well—for both, Harijans and others. But in 1957, such a two-member constituency gave maximum votes

to two Harijans both of whom were declared duly elected. The country applauded this double success of Harijans; but the Congress, whose general candidate, V.V. Giri, had lost, thought otherwise. It now reserved only some single member constituencies—depriving the Harijans of a wider base of Harijan electorate, and depriving non-SC of non-SC representative in those reserved constituencies.

On another count also, the SC and ST could have a grievance. While they get the seats reserved for them in the Lower Houses under the Constitution, no party has thought fit to bring them to the Upper Houses, where there is no reservation, in any significant numbers.

However, the issue of reservation of admission and jobs stands on a very different footing. While the Constitution makes reservation of seats in legislative bodies mandatory—albeit for ten years at a time—it speaks of only SC and ST claim to services and posts in connection with the affairs of the Union or of a State. Actually, in practice, it has become as mandatory as the former—and that too for an indefinite period, with not even a 10-year review of the policy.

This percentage has not only been raised from time to time, it has been extended to public sector enterprises, colleges and even research laboratories. Seats which can't be filled in one year, can be carried forward for three years. And reservation applies not only to initial recruitment but also to subsequent promotions. And so a SC or ST man can become the boss of his other colleagues, who had scored better than him, to begin with. All this has led to much bitterness in government offices.

On top of this has come the Mandal Report giving 27 per cent reservation to Other Backward Classes, all of which puts merit at a discount.

The anti-reservations case, in brief, is that there are too many reservations, that there should be no reservation in promotions, that families which have made good, should not continue to profit by reservations and that there should be no reservation for OBCs.

The problem is multilateral and it needs to be considered dis-

passionately. The real mischief here is not reservations but the politics of reservation. From time to time particularly on election-eve, government announces more jobs for SC and ST. This irritates the unemployed youth of other castes. But SC and ST youth also feel cheated, because they continue to be under-represented in all but class IV jobs. The three-year carry forward rule is quite pointless, because enough men are not found to fill the reserved jobs even for one year! The anti-reservationists, however, do have a case against reservations in promotion; even the British never did that, not even for Muslims.

They have an even stronger case on well-to-do SC and ST families cornering seats and jobs. The argument is that only the poor and underprivileged among SC and ST should enjoy these reservations. Perhaps it will be a good idea to 'unschedule' the families of SC and ST men who become State or Central legislators, or Class I or II officers or those who are prosperous enough to be paying income tax. Such an arrangement will leave these openings to the really poor and deprived among SC and ST, and help them come up, which is the true intent of reservations. Even Thakkar Bapa, Gandhiji's chief lieutenant in Harijan uplift, had urged phasing out of developed castes from the mass of Harijans who still needed special scholarships and reserved jobs.

Also there are other anomalies in the reservation policy that need to be sorted out. If a Harijan becomes a Sikh, he is still recognised as SC: but if he becomes a Buddhist he ceases to be recognised as SC! This is wrong. All Harijans governed by Hindu Law must be recognised as SC.

And this law should apply to ST also. Such ST as go out of the Hindu pale, should cease to be recognised as ST. Today the position is that STs converted to Christianity are not only profiting by foreign charity, they are also cornering all the facilities offered by Central and State governments. This, in turn, is putting a premium on conversions, which constitute a potential threat to the unity, integrity and peace of the land.

Another anomaly of this system is that certain castes and tribes have been included in the Schedules not because they are

poor and backward but because they are influential. And so ever since Raj Bahadur, the then union minister, got the well off tribe of Meenas 'scheduled', to secure his Bharatpur seat, the Meenas have cornered most of the facilities, leaving poor tribals like the Bhils high and dry!

Yet another anomaly obtains in the treatment of Vanavasis and Girijans. While tribals in the rest of the country, if rich, pay income tax, tribals in the northeast, however rich, are exempt from it! Outside Bombay city, there is probably a higher percentage of multi-millionaires in Nagaland and Mizoram, Meghalaya and Manipur than anywhere else in the country—thanks to official pampering of rebels and missionaries. This discrimination must end. All those with taxable incomes must pay income tax.

Once these anomalies are sorted out there will be less pressure for the extension and elaboration of reservations. And there will be greater recognition of the fact that many traditionally 'service communities' have no land which many OBCs have; that many OBCs are very well represented in the police and armed forces: and that if tribals can be as poor as Shabari in *Ramayana*, even Brahmins can be as poor as Sudama in *Shrimad Bhagvad*.

The real trouble here is not with reservations, rationally conceived and justly executed, but with the politics of reservation. It was because Madhav Singh Solanki in Gujarat increased OBC reservations from 10 per cent to 28 per cent on the eve of the 1985 elections that the fat was in the fire. The result was hundreds of lives lost and hundreds of crores of rupees worth of property destroyed. NTR, not to be left behind, added 40 new OBCs to the existing list of 102—and raised their reservation from 25 per cent to 44 per cent! It is these politicians who forge KHAM and AJGAR and now even MAJGAR!—a gang-up of certain groupings to capture power—who are a major menace to the peace and progress of society.

Government could, and should, call an all-party meeting to consider all these issues coolly and thoroughly. There is a feeling that while all parties swear by more and more reservations, all of them have serious reservations about this policy. It is significant that though Congress swore by the Mandal Report submitted in 1980, neither the mother nor the son implemented it in nine long years! And it is no less significant that Deputy Prime Minister Devi Lal and Janata Dal leader Chandra Shekhar have openly sympathised with the anti-reservationists. Let there be a national consensus on this issue free from partisan one-up-manship.

The basic considerations here are two: the unity of the people and the upliftment of the poor. Reservations were started as relief for the underprivileged to make for sounder national unity. Actually it has degenerated into a policy of grab. A functionally organised society has in the process tended to be fractured. Reservations, provided as crutches, have become sticks with which to beat your opponent. The earlier Indian tendency was 'Sanskritisation' in which every caste tried to rise higher. An unimaginative reservation policy threatens not only to perpetuate caste but also pits caste against caste as each tries to outmanoeuvre to claim deprived status. This whole sickly trend has to be reversed.

Secondly, jobs by themselves can never uplift the poor. After all how many jobs can be there? The important thing is that the economy is buoyed up—and reorganised to maximise employment. It is no use depriving lakhs of weavers of their work through a synthetic fibre-inspired textile policy—and then throwing some jobs at them like so many crumbs. Indeed the commitment of BJP and some other parties to 'right to work' can never materialise unless it is made part of a decentralised labour-intensive industry. □

Women's Priorities

Women care fifty times more for a marriage than a ministry.

—Bagehot

Women viewed pilgrimage as alternative to marriage.

—Theodore Zeldin

Solving the Kashmir Problem

Ek Desh mein Do Vidhan
Ek Desh mein Do Pradhan
Ek Desh mein do Nishan
Nahin Chalenge, Nahin Chalenge

—Praja Parishad slogan

The question is often asked: How will the BJP solve the Kashmir problem?

That question was answered by a Kashmiri extremist a few years back. He told a surprised Ms. Tavleen Singh that only the BJP could solve the Kashmir problem.

The reason for that is simple; only BJP has had a clear and consistent view of the Kashmir problem all these years.

The BJP has no doubt that the Kashmir problem has been bungled all along. It was wrong to make an indefinite promise of a Plebiscite when the people were very much with us, warning the Pakistani raiders:

Hamlawar Ho Khabardar:
Hum Kashmiri Hain Tayar.

It was very wrong to refer the matter to a UN torn by super-power rivalries. It was very wrong to complain of a dispute in Kashmir—and not of aggression in Kashmir. And it was again very wrong to cease-fire in Kashmir at a time when the raiders were on the run and we could have easily cleared the whole State right up to Karakoram Pass bordering China. Pakistan would not have dared

to confront us because, as General Cariappa once told me, in 1947, it had a grand total of eight tanks and, in the event of an Indo-Pak war in 1947-48, our Army's first halt would have been at Attock, on the River Indus.

Nor did our follies end there. We introduced Article 370 in the Constitution, giving a special separate and separatist status to Jammu and Kashmir State. It was this "special status" that planted the idea of an Independent Kashmir in the mind of some Kashmiris.

The Sangh Parivar wholly disapproved of all these false moves. In 1952 the Praja Parishad launched a movement for full integration of the State. Its historic slogan was: *Ek Desh Mein Do Vidhan, Ek Desh Mein Do Pradhan, Ek Desh Mein Do Nishan—Nahin Chalenge, Nahin Chalenge* (We cannot allow two Constitutions, two Heads of State and two Flags in one country). Jana Sangh supported the Praja Parishad movement and a big *Satyagraha* followed in Jammu, Delhi, Jalandhar and Pathankot. Dr. Shyama Prasad Mukherji, BJS President, died in detention in Srinagar in suspicious circumstances. Soon after, Government of India dismissed and detained Sheikh Abdullah.

Bakshi Ghulam Mohammed stabilised the Kashmir situation. But once again there was no clarity on the Government side. There was only piecemeal integration. Instead of honestly deleting the separatist Article 370, as suggested by Bakshi, Pandit Nehru said "it will erode away". Constitutions may be amended where necessary; they don't have to be eroded. Erosion is as bad for Constitutions as it is for soil.

And then came Mr. Nehru's mysterious 'Kamaraj Plan'. Among those sent out of office was Bakshi. The exit of this strong man as Chief Minister of J & K State encouraged Pakistan to play games in Kashmir. The result was the Indo-Pak War of 1965. The decisive War of 1971 put Pakistan in its place. We had partitioned Pakistan and taken over 90,000 Pakistani Prisoners of War. But while the soldiers won the war, the politicians lost the peace. They returned the POWs on only an oral undertaking by Bhutto that Pakistan would never again raise the Kashmir issue.

Even so, things continued smoothly enough. There was not much of a Kashmir problem when Mrs. Gandhi came back to power in 1980. But before long she had lawlessly dismissed Dr. Farooq Abdullah and installed the corrupt and communal G.M. Shah. Later she re-instated Farooq but forced on him a coalition with the Congress. That reduced Farooq to the role of a puppet of Delhi in Kashmiri eyes. In the elections that preceded the coalition, there was shameless rigging by the Government. It was in this silly situation that Pakistan played on the people's hurt feelings and caused the crisis of the last few years.

The V.P. Singh Government capitulated to the extremists when it released notorious terrorists to secure the release of Rubaiya, daughter of then Union Home Minister Mufti, against the wishes of Farooq. He should have known that terrorists would not dare to do any harm to Rubaiya—and stood firm.

Today life is normal in Kashmir. Tourism is up, terrorism is down. Schools, colleges, hospitals, offices, cinemas, bazaars, are functioning normally. The media does not report all this. But as and when there is any act of terrorism, inspired by Pakistan, it gets page one coverage and people think things are just too bad in Kashmir.

The BJP is convinced that the 'temporary and transitional' Article 370 must go. But it can go only when there is a two-thirds majority for it in the Parliament. That is going to take some time. And BJP would avail of this time to convince everybody, and particularly the Kashmiris, that Article 370 is not good for anybody. It has only acted as a cover for corruption and irresponsibility. Once it is gone, Kashmir will have the same rights and responsibilities as Punjab and Bengal.

The BJP will make it clear that the accession of the State is complete and final and that Kashmir is not going anywhere. To this end, law and order will be restored at the earliest. The State could be given a unified command of civil and military powers. There could be a call for surrender of all illegal arms—on pain of confiscation of property. The Indo-Pakistan border could be sealed with land mines to prevent all illegal movements. There could even

be counter-guerilla groups to take care of pro-Pakistani guerilla groups.

Simultaneously Kashmiris should be put wise about what would have happened to them, had they opted for Pakistan in 1947. The Valley would have been inundated by Punjabis and Pathans. Kashmir would have ceased to be Kashmiri—even as Sindh has half ceased to be Sindhi.

People must be assured that as soon as order is restored, there will be elections and that these elections will be fully free and fair. Sheikh Abdullah used to say that the only time Kashmir had fair elections was in 1977 when Janata Government was in power in Delhi. Anybody contesting elections has to swear loyalty to the Constitution. If, therefore, anybody does anything unconstitutional, the law will take care of him. For the rest, people can have the Government of their choice. There shall be no rigging of polls—as has too often been the case so far.

Much of the mischief in Kashmir has been created by schools run by U.P. *maulvis* on behalf of the State unit of the Jamaat-e-Islami, which is affiliated to the Jamaat in Pakistan. These schools have been manufacturing Pakistanis out of Kashmiris. These people have renamed five hundred towns, renaming Anantnag as 'Islamabad'. This Jamaat must be banned, its schools be taken over by the Government and its U.P. *maulvis* sent back home.

The Jammu & Kashmir State today consists of Jammu, Kashmir and Ladakh. The three areas are geographically and linguistically distinct and different. New Delhi could, therefore, consider reorganising the State into three administrative units, to give them all a greater sense of identity and autonomy.

Today though Kashmiri language is recognised by the Indian Constitution in its Eighth Schedule, it is not the language either of education or of administration. That role goes to Urdu and English. A major reason for this is that Jammu would not accept Kashmiri and Kashmir would not accept Dogri or Hindi. So they compromise on Urdu. If, as and when Kashmir Valley is set up as a State, Kashmiri must be introduced as the medium of instruction and administration. That alone will strengthen and revive Kashmiriat

and checkmate the appeal and influence of Pakistan. Government has been quite unimaginative in touting Akbar in Kashmir as the model of secularism. Kashmiris look upon Akbar as an invader who extinguished Kashmiri autonomy. Only a revival of Kashmiri language and Kashmiriat can reinforce the wholesome Kashmiri tradition of Sufi saints and poets.

If Pakistan does not like all this and creates problems we should be prepared to give it a bloody nose.

It must be clearly understood that national frontiers are defended, and not debated. And any compromise on this score will only compromise the unity, integrity and independence of India.

□

Kashmir Problem is ISI-CIA

Pakistan says it feels incomplete without Kashmir. I say India feels incomplete without Pakistan.

—A.B. Vajpayee

Even Sheikh Abdullah was opposed to Article 370.

—L.K. Advani

BBC refers to Kashmir as India-controlled. Why does it not refer to northern Ireland as Britain-controlled?

—Vigilante

Kashmir always belonged to India.

—Dr. Parvez & Dr. Inayatullah
Pakistan Scholars

USA desires continued Jammu & Kashmir militancy.

—P.V. Narasimha Rao
(30.11.1995)

Fundamentalists are agents of the West.

—Benazir Bhutto
(2.12.1995)

The Bangla Flood

Is it Grow More Food,
or Grow More Muslims?

—Lord Wavell

When Bankim penned his patriotic song, *Vande Mataram*, he invoked seven crore (*Sapta Koti*) Bengalis. Today East Bengal alone has a population of twelve crore. The Bangladeshi numbers have been growing at a rate that can only alarm India.

There are one lakh Bangladeshis in Delhi alone. According to 'Dhaka Courier' this number is not less than one and a half lakh in East Delhi alone. The unofficial figure for Delhi is something like four lakh. In the country as a whole, the Bangladeshi number is well above one crore.

That Muslim 'East Pakistan' should have squeezed out millions of Hindus was bad enough. This had caused Sardar Patel to demand of Pakistan land to settle these refugees. And had the great man lived a few years more, he would no doubt have secured justice for Bengali Hindu refugees. However, with his death in 1950, those hopes were dashed to pieces. And for several years now, even Bangla Muslims have been pouring into India. For example, in the first six months of 1991, some 39,055 infiltrators were intercepted on the West Bengal border; and it was found that 28,000—some 75 per cent—of them were Muslims.

I would not say they are infiltrators in the sense that they are coming here to create trouble. But they are certainly infiltrators in the sense that they are coming illegally—and they don't have the

grievance of Bangla Hindus, namely that they are being discriminated against. They are coming by the million because economic conditions are much better here.

However, their coming can only strain and depress the Indian economy. And in any case they have no right to come.

Until Independence/Partition, East Bengal Muslims used to overflow into Assam. The British had permitted anybody travelling from anywhere in East Bengal to anywhere in Assam on payment of a railway fare of six *annas* only. This had given rise to Assamese-Bengali tensions in Assam. When Saadullah, Muslim League leader—who became Prime Minister of Assam following the resignation of Congress ministries in 1940—he again imported large numbers of Bengali Muslim farm labourers, on the excuse of 'grow more food' campaign. Lord Wavell, then Viceroy, was driven to describe the policy as 'Grow More Muslims'.

After Partition this human flood stopped. But in the last several years this flood has become a raging tide.

Had East Bengal continued to be part of the Indian state, its people would have had the constitutional right to settle in other states—so long as they did not disturb the social balance there. But with the partition of Bengal and the secession of East Bengal from the Indian Union, they have no right, legal or moral, to enter our territory in any number. Their successful inundation is due to two factors: it is not easy to stop the movement of people across the fields; and the erstwhile government was not even interested in stopping immigrants, who were viewed as sure Congress voters. However, what are votes for the Congress, is a problem for the country.

Of late the infiltrators have become so cheeky that they have even formed a Bangladesh Mohajir Sangh in West Bengal. In a recent demonstration in Calcutta, they demanded Indian citizenship as their right.

Meanwhile, some pseudo-intellectuals of Bangladesh have come up with the argument of a 'globalised manpower market' in a 'new demographic order', to demand lebensraum (living space) for their surplus population. No country has a right to breed beyond the limits of its physical resources and then demand more and more land or opportunities from other countries. If Bangladesh must produce more children than it can feed—its per capita income is less than half that of India—let it go and seek land in Australia, Africa or South America; it cannot strain Indian patience beyond our limits of toleration.

Already the Bangladeshi presence has generated many serious tensions. In the North-east, it has caused all the seven states to assert their separateness, in a bid to preserve their respective identity. It has also led to massive violence, as in Nellie a few years ago. In some districts of Bihar, Bangladeshi Muslims have displaced even local Muslims. Since the immigrants gladly accept lower wages, it has become impossible to enforce the Minimum Farm Labour Wages Act.

Of late even Delhi and Bombay have felt the pressure of this immigration. The government must identify Bangla Muslims who can't prove their Indian citizenship on January 26, 1950—when the Indian Constitution was adopted—and repatriate them to their native land.

Although the prime responsibility for this situation is that of the government and people of Bangladesh, Congressmen, communists and some pseudo-intellectuals also cannot escape their share of responsibility. While politicians have been thinking only of votes, these intellectuals have been conjuring dreams of the 'Bangaliat' of all Bengalis. It was in this dreamy state that East Bengal Hindu refugees did not ask for an Evacuee Property Law to cover their property losses in East Pakistan. And it is this same wishful thinking that persuades them to overlook the Bangla inundation. This is the dreamy stuff, of which the July 1947 Sarat-Suhrawardy scheme of a 'United Independent Bengal' was made. It is about time the dreamy Bengal intellectual woke up to the cruel reality of partition of Bengal—and of India. For, this Bangla infiltration is something more than a nuisance; it is a menace.

□

Prime Ministers vs. Presidents

Nehru, Indira, Rajiv had problems with Rajendra Babu, Radhakrishnan, Zail Singh.

Mr. Zail Singh made much news as President.

This was not the first time that the Prime Minister and the President have had an argument; only, the latest is also the loudest argument between our Head of State and Head of Government. And I suspect the quarrel is inherent in the Constitution. The Constitution gives us the leader of the majority party in the Lok Sabha as Prime Minister. But it also gives us a President elected by all the legislators in the country. The fact that the latter can be impeached, assumes that he can do many things, some of which may turn out not to be to the liking of the majority party. Mr. Setalvad, first Attorney-General of India, said the President could not refuse assent to bills or criticise the government publicly, but he could influence legislation by his advice. He could not dismiss a Minister—except on the advice of the Prime Minister—but that in special circumstances, he could dismiss the Prime Minister, dissolve the House and order fresh elections. Among constitutional Pundits, Alladi Krishnaswami, Gopalaswamy Ayyangar and Ambedkar felt that the President was a titular head; but B.N. Rau, K.M. Munshi and K. Santhanam held that the President had very substantial powers. In this situation, a clash between the President and the Prime Minister can be avoided only by having an elder statesman, a man of stature and quality, as President—and listening to his sage advice with due deference. But the trouble is that Nehru

and his progeny as Prime Ministers tried to use the President as a rubber stamp. Since no self-respecting man would act as a rubber-stamp, they tried to install rubber-stamps as Presidents. But, such is the substance of the presidential office that, after some time, even these rubber-stamps began to act as men. And that horrified the dynastic Premiers. The President-Premier dissonance, therefore, has been a regular feature of the Indian political scene.

The whole thing began right in the beginning: Nehru did not want Rajendra Prasad as the first President; he wanted C.R. But be it said to his credit that when he found the Party overwhelmingly for Rajen Babu, he fell in line. But he never gave him due respect. The very first thing he did was to give him a secretary, who was more of a spy on him. This secretary in his memoirs depicted this scholar-statesman-sage, as if he were a village idiot.

When Sardar Patel died in Bombay, Nehru told Prasad—and his Cabinet colleagues—not to attend his funeral. Rajendra Prasad had no choice but to defy the Prime Minister and go and pay his respects to the sacred memory of Sardar Patel. When it was decided to rebuild the historic Somnath temple, Nehru again asked Prasad not to attend the ceremony. And once again Rajendra Prasad had to respect national sentiment and defy Nehru's diktat. While Nehru always attended a Kumbh Mela to win popularity among the masses, he objected to the President washing the feet of Kashi Pandits. The quiet and dignified Rajen Babu told the haughty Nehru that even the high and mighty must bow to spiritual leaders. President Eisenhower of the US and Queen Elizabeth II of England repeatedly invited Rajendra Prasad to visit their respective countries, but Nehru would not let him do so! (Rajiv was only following in his grandfather's footsteps when he vetoed Zail Singh's state visits to other countries.) Interestingly enough, Nehru himself went to Washington to *salaam* the US President on the eve of every Indian General Election!

In 1957 again, Nehru opposed a second term for Prasad. He even sounded out the four Chief Ministers from the South to demand a President from that region—to keep out Prasad. But they did not bite his CR bait. Nehru, therefore, inspired a few columnists

from the South to demand a President from there. But once again, the then healthy Congress party opted for Prasad—and Nehru again fell in line. But he continued his cold war on the President. He would announce senior appointments—and Prasad would learn about them from the Press. Rajen Babu could be very meek, but he was nobody's fool. He once told Nehru: "You are setting bad precedents. A President who did not like you, could give you a lot of trouble."

Meanwhile, it was only the Prime Minister giving trouble to the President. And so on November 28, 1960, Dr. Rajendra Prasad made a historic statement. In his address to the Indian Law Institute, he suggested that the Supreme Court define the respective functions of the President and the Prime Minister. When Nehru learnt in advance of the contents of this speech, he arrived for the function unannounced. Though the President addressed the Institute, printed copies of his speech were not distributed; they were returned to Rashtrapati Bhavan!

It is sad to say that Nehru carried his animus against Prasad—as also against Patel—even after death. He not only failed to attend Rajen Babu's cremation in Patna in 1963, he asked the new President, Dr. Radhakrishnan, also not to attend it! Once again it was the President who showed good taste and told him: "No, I think I must go and attend the funeral. The respect is due to him and must be paid."

Although Dr. Radhakrishnan was Nehru's own special choice, mutual disillusionment was not long in coming. After the Chinese attack, the President was even thinking of replacing Nehru by a Government of national consensus. Also the President viewed Nehru's Kamaraj Plan with dismay. When Indira became Prime Minister she still remembered her father's uneasy relationship with Dr. Radhakrishnan. She therefore, refused to give him a second term although her own benefactor, Kamaraj, asked for it.

She now decided to have lesser men for President. Her first choice was Dr. Zakir Hussain, a gentleman scholar. When Dr. Hussain was Governor of Bihar, one of his grand-daughters fell in love with a Police Officer, Mr. Mishra. Dr. Hussain insisted that

Mishra Jr. embrace Islam, if he wanted to be his grandson-in-law. The young man obliged and became 'Mishra Khan'.

1967 was the year when the Congress was out of power all the way from Amritsar to Calcutta. The entire Opposition—from CPI to BJS—put up the erstwhile Chief Justice of India, Subba Rao. But Ms Gandhi did not have any consultations with the Opposition. She whipped her party into voting for Zakir Hussain, who won by a small margin.

Dr. Zakir Hussain did well after his election to pay respects to the *Swami* of Shringeri Math. But he once again raised a controversy when another of his grand-daughters fell in love with his ADC from Kerala. He also succeeded in having him converted to Islam.

Dr. Zakir Hussain died within two years of his Presidency. The ruling party put up Sanjiva Reddy; but Ms Gandhi sabotaged his election and got V.V. Giri elected.

Giri came to be known as a rubber-stamp. But soon she fell out even with her rubber-stamp. When Giri told IAS officers in Lucknow, not to hesitate to arrest corrupt businessmen, she asked him to have his speeches approved by her. The old trade unionist in Giri retorted that he was not prepared to show her any of his speeches, except the ones he made while opening a new session of Parliament. She kept him in leash by first promising him a second term, then a ministership for his son, and ultimately leaving Giri Jr. a simple MP. Giri died a disenchanted man.

Fakhruddin's term was cut short by death during the Emergency. He had kept a diary but it was never published.

Sanjiva Reddy had an uneasy equation with Morarjibhai. And Zail Singh had a stormy relationship with Rajiv. Fortunately Venkatraman, Sharma and Narayanan have had a pleasant relationship with their Prime Ministers.

□

Case for National Government

We are all children of Bharat Mata and products of Twentieth Century.

Even while Mr. V.P. Singh was forming his minority Government, some thinking people were considering a majority and even a national Government. In fact, Mr. A.B. Vajpayee mooted the idea of a national government—a government of national unity and national consensus, a government of cooperation and not of confrontation. It is but natural that nationalists should think in national terms.

It is a matter of satisfaction that Mr. V.P. Singh, Mr. Chandra Shekhar and Mr. Devi Lal generally welcomed the idea in principle. And even the Congress(I) spokesman said his party would consider the idea if it came from the President. In fact, many in the country were pleased by the idea of a government of national unity. It is so much in tune with the national ethos and the tradition of integration.

The case for a national government is easily stated. Under our first-past-the-post electoral system, a party with even less than 50 per cent of the vote can easily collect 75 per cent of the seats and then exercise 100 per cent power. The whole thing is democratic in form but undemocratic in spirit. In the USA, such a system is corrected by various committees of the two Houses, which are bipartisan and very powerful. They can veto the President's proposals, and even his appointments.

However, there is no such scope in India. Our various

parliamentary consultative committees are talking shops with no power at all. The new Standing Committees of various deparments are not much better. As a result some 50 per cent of the Indian people, who did not vote for the party in power, always feel cheated. There is no empathy between half the population and the Government, which even goes so far as to starve Opposition constituencies and shower patronage on VIP constituencies. The Prime Minister's constituency gets a regular bonanza of a whole lot of goodies. Opposition voters return the compliment; they generally find fault with the Government when anything goes wrong. The result is party warfare for much of the time.

This is an unhappy state of affairs. A broad-based national government would give a sense of satisfaction and participation to *all* the people. It could make for all-round cooperation and, as a result, for quicker and better development.

Since no party has a surfeit of talent, a national government could have the best talents from all the parties. In such a government, everybody will be on his best behaviour, competing in excellence and integrity. Much of the corruption so far has been due to the fact that we have had a one-man party and a one-party Government. But imagine a national government that includes BJP, Congress and Communists. Would it tolerate commissions and kickbacks? Every minister—and, therefore, every bureaucrat—would put his best foot forward.

The question is: Will there be any Opposition in such a system? If some groups do not join such a government, they would obviously be in the Opposition. For the rest, while all members of Parliament would be free to state their views on different matters, those who back the national government would stand by it all at the time of voting in the House. Such a national government would be at once an all-party and partyless affair. All, or almost all, parties would be represented, but they would not work in a partisan manner.

It might be asked: How can the BJP and Communists join the same Government? This is a legitimate question because both parties have so far taken the position that they will not support a

government that includes the other. However, at a time when the Berlin Wall has fallen down, and even Communist countries are discarding one-party governments, such a cooperative attitude cannot be ruled out. If only people free themselves from the prison-house of their own cliches and pet theories, they will see Indian reality in a very different light.

Even as early as 1967, when the Jana Sangh and Communists worked together in the coalition governments of Punjab, Uttar Pradesh and Bihar, they had no problem among themselves. In the new century, they can try the experiments at the Central level. In 1968, these State coalition governments were toppled by a hostile Congress Centre; a coalition Government at the Centre will have no such fear of being toppled.

Today, the Communists dub the BJP 'communal', and the latter return the 'anti-national' compliment. But these are only pejorative terms, words of abuse, employed without cool consideration or proper cerebration. Words are thrown about like stones. There could be a ceasefire in this verbal warfare. After all, we are all children of Bharat Mata—and products of the 20th century.

Assuming the parties did come together and formed a national government, how would they face the next election? Parties could put up their candidates where they liked; they could fight the elections as sportsmen compete for honours. Since they know that they would be working together in the next national government, there would be no acrimony, no hard feelings. They could contest elections as friends—and they could then work together in a national government as brothers. Party warfare is alien to the Indian character; the Indian tradition is Synthesis, *Sangam*, *Yogam*.

It is significant that most democratic countries today have multi-party governments. In the USA, the President, the Senate and the House often belong to different parties, but major policies—and even key appointments—are bipartisan. Japan not only has a multi-party government, amendments moved by parties in the Opposition are treated with respect—and often accepted, at least in part.

The United Kingdom has had national governments

consisting of both the major parties, not only during war but also in peacetime. For example, after the Great Depression of 1929, when the UK went off the Gold Standard, the Conservative Party joined hands with the Labour Prime Minister, Ramsay MacDonald, to give the country a broadbased government in a time of crisis. India, with its great and growing problems, is in a continuing crisis; it needs a national government on a regular basis.

It is happy to note that independent India also began its career with a national government, with the blessings of Mahatma Gandhi. Half the first Nehru Cabinet in 1947 comprised non-Congressmen. There were luminaries like Dr. Shyama Prasad Mukherji and Dr. Ambedkar, Shanmugam Chetty and Homi Bhabha, John Matthai, K. C. Neogy and Baldev Singh. It was the best government in living memory.

It is a comforting thought that many people are thinking along these lines. Mr. C. Subramaniam, veteran leader from Tamil Nadu, suggested a 'National Government of All Talents'. He also felt that political parties should not go 'for each other's jugular', and suggested that they shed their 'hatreds and antagonisms'. There could then be a 'Standing Consultative Body of all parties represented in Parliament, working together with mutual goodwill and advising the Government on policies and issues aimed at furthering the national interest.'

□

Shivaji The Nation-Builder

Society is a partnership of the living, the dead and the unborn.

—Burke

Who controls the past, controls the future, who controls the present controls the past.

—George Orwell

Shivaji proved by his example that the Hindu race can build a nation, found a state and rise to the full stature of their growth.

—Jadunath Sarkar

III. ECONOMY

The West versus the Rest

There's a story about the golden rule:
he who has gold, rules.

—*Boss Hurwitz*

Multinational Corporations are all the time saying that they do not have level playing field in India—and that justice and WTO alike demand that they get it. On the other hand Indian Businessmen—at first of Bombay Club and now of All India Club—also feel that they are not having level playing field *vis-a-vis* MNCs and that they must be protected from the Wild-West cow-boy approach of MNCs. It is good to note that both sides want level playing field. It should, therefore, be possible to examine where, and to what extent, the ground is not level—and for whom—and how it may be levelled.

The situation is reminiscent of the dialogue between Alexander and King Porus of India. Porus wondered aloud why Alexander had entered India. And he made a very fair offer to him: he said that let the two of them declare their gold and silver, and whoever had less of it may be given some to equalise their wealth. Porus, however, entered a caveat. If, he said, Alexander had come to divert and take away the river waters—"vital national interests"—there would be war. Although Western historians have unilaterally declared Alexander victor, when the war ended, Porus was a bigger king than before!

Now Indian Business certainly has certain advantages in India. They know the country and the people. They know their workers, their managers and their consumers. And they know their government. However, these are advantages enjoyed by every business on its respective home ground. These advantages, therefore, cancel themselves out.

We also have the advantage of the Sun, which causes the crops—and even humans—to mature faster. But this again is cancelled out by the cold climate enjoyed by MNCs in the North where, for that very reason, people can work harder.

We also have the advantage of cheaper labour; but this labour is not as skilled as in the West. And in any case we have to employ much more labour than they. Also, when an MNC starts manufacturing in India, it too gets the advantage of cheaper labour.

In addition, Indian Business did, for years, have the protection of import substitution and high tariff walls. However, today, these walls have been all but pulled down. So much so that, to give just one example, today many steel mills in India, big and small—have had to close down because of cheaper imports. But on the other hand the big foreign companies—the MNCs—have tremendous—even over-whelming advantages. To treat Indian and these foreign companies at par would be like throwing the lamb to the wolves—in the name of 'freedom' and 'equality'.

Because the West has dominated the world for the last two centuries, its domination shows in every sphere. Since it has more wealth and more capital, interest rates are much lower in the West. While an American MNC may have to pay only 5% interest, an Indian company has to pay 15%.

The same with technology. The West is not only ahead of us in technology, it often refuses to sell the state-of-the-art technology to us. USA not only refused to sell cryogenic engines to us; it pressed Russia not to sell them to us!

Although much of the oil comes from the Persian Gulf area, world oil prices are determined by adding what it would cost to transport this oil to Texas, in the Gulf of Mexico, and using it as the base price! No wonder oil is cheaper in USA than in India, though these oilwells are much nearer to India than USA. All this jugglery is possible only because American—and some other

western—oil companies control the world oil trade.

These companies even organised the oil crisis of 1970's, to raise oil prices high and earn oil super-profits. These oil profits were then used by the World Bank as a bait to tempt developing countries to borrow money by the billion—and so walk into debt-traps. In the Seventies the developing world's foreign debt was $ 21 billion; in the Nineties it rose to $ 110 billion. During the same period even oil exporting countries', foreign debt went up to $ 390 billion! As a robber-baron of the West, engaged in felling even great 1000-year old trees, put it candidly; "There's a story about the golden rule. He who has gold, rules."

Nor is this Western predominance confined to the material factors of production. It is, if anything, even more pervasive in the non-physical factors of economic life. Today we are living in a world of instant communications and informatics. And here again the West is miles ahead of us. There are not only more Western satellites in orbit monitoring the world—and its marine and underground resources—Western electronic media is penetrating every nook and corner of the globe. It is influencing not only economic choices but also tastes and values. The Western advertising blitz is pushing Western products. Today even Delhi police station name-boards carry Pepsi advertisements. When developing countries refuse tobacco ads, these MNCs sponsor sports events to promote their smoking message. And so while smoking is going down in the US—because of its known carcinogenic properties—tobacco company profits are going up! Mr. Lawrence Summers, chief economist of the World Bank openly advocated that polluting industries and garbage be dumped in developing countries.

In the name of a 'level playing field', American banks have set up shop in India. But they never fulfil the social responsibilities shouldered by Indian banks, which latter have to open branches in rural areas and give loans on concessional terms to agriculture, small scale industry and cooperatives.

This inequality shows even in the realm of law. Foreign companies coming to India do not want to be judged by Indian law;

they invoke the law in a third country! And so the Enron dispute is going to British courts. In simple words the level playing field of MNCs amounts to 'heads we win and tails you lose'.

The West has not only more guns and more gold—and even more grain in a hungry world—with which to dominate the world, all the powerful international organisations—UNO, World Bank, International Monetary Fund, World Trade Organisation, International Court of Justice, ILO, FAO—are based in the West and captive to the West. As Samuel P. Huntington of Harvard candidly puts it: "Through the IMF and other international economic institutions, the West promotes its economic interests and imposes on other nations the economic policies it thinks appropriate." This leads to resentment and the emergence of a conflict between 'the West and the Rest'. And so Prof. Huntington concedes: "In any poll of non-Western peoples, the IMF undoubtedly would win the support of Finance Ministers and a few others, but get an overwhelmingly unfavourable rating from just about everyone else" (*vide* Foreign Affairs Quarterly, Summer 1993). But instead of redressing the grievances of the South, Huntington wants "the West to maintain the economic and military power necessary to protect its interests in relation to these civilizations." This is the reason why USA did not want India to go nuclear or develop a missile capability. If India developed military muscle, the West would not be able to twist our arms and extract more and more concessions from us for its MNCs. It will thus be seen that, in the booming name of 'globalisation', the West is only trying to perpetuate its hegemony of the World. It is gobble-isation. When nationalist India responds to the challenge of globalisation with the clarion call of *Swadeshi*, it is not doing so to ply the *Charkha*; it is doing so only to protect its independence, identity and integrity, ensure its growth and secure a proper place in the comity of nations.

Coming back to the economic domain, we don't have to be taken in by the glib talk of 'free trade'. Just as roads need speed-breakers, developing economies need protection. A hundred years back when Britain asked USA to abolish its tariff walls and engage in free trade, then US President Ulysses Grant reminded them that

UK had protected its industries for a hundred years before launching out on free trade. USA, said Grant, would also do the same after hundred years. And so may we—in the fullness of time! Actually, even today, USA gives much higher subsidies to Agriculture than India, and it has any number of import quotas.

Keynes, the man who, with his integral economic thinking, helped pull the world out of the morass of the Great Depression, has said: "I sympathise, therefore, with those who would minimise, rather than those who would maximise, economic entanglements between nations." (*vide* David C. Korten: 'When Corporations Rule the World', Earthscan, London, 1996). And those who want India to join the league of Asian tigers would do well to remember that Japan and Korea, Taiwan and Singapore did not attain their leonine status through *laissez faire* and free trade! □

The Global Trap

World-class dreams are at home in San Francisco's Fairmont Hotel. It is icon and institution, a luxury inn with a legendary *joie de vivre*.

The Fairmont pragmatists sum up the future in a pair of numbers and a concept: '20 to 80'. Only twenty per cent will get employment. And the rest? Will 80 per cent of those willing to work be left without a job? 'Sure', says the American writer Jeremy Rifkin, author of 'The End of Work'. These 80% will get a dole—and left to entertain themselves with tits i.e. teats.

The expression on everyone's lips is Zbigniew Brzezinski's 'tittytainment'. The old Polish-born warhorse, who was Jimmy Carter's national security adviser for four years, thinks of 'tittytainment' ('Tits' plus 'entertainment'). Perhaps a mixture of deadening entertainment and adequate nourishment will keep the world's frustrated population in relatively good spirits.

—'The Global Trap'
by Hans Peter Martin & Herald Schuman
(Zed Books, London)

Globalisation Gone Mad

Market fundamentalism is today a greater threat to open society than any totalitarian ideology.

—George Soros

Recently an Hon'ble Minister came out with his 'Ten Commandments' for privatisation of Public Sector Undertakings. Actually his ten commandments add up to only One Commandment namely that the Public Sector is no good and that it should be wound up and privatised as much and as fast as possible.

Briefly put, the minister's case is that lot of money is locked up in PSUs, and their privatisation will release lot of money, with which we could retire Public Debt and invest more in the Social Sector; privatisation, he says, will make the economy more productive and competitive and improve its quality; it will also help us with exports in the World Market; it will eliminate bureaucratisation; it will also cut subsidies and generate more revenue for the Government; it will make shares in the privatised PSUs available to the common man; and it will generate employment.

Every single argument for Disinvestment above is, at best, a half-truth. Every business locks up resources, whether these resources are private or public. When we privatise a PSU, we do not create new capital or set up a new industry. We just paste a new label on an old industry.

Disinvestment has gone on for almost ten years now. Let the

Government inform the country how much Public Debt has been retired with the sale proceeds of PSUs—and how much of these proceeds has gone to finance the 'Social Sector'. It is public knowledge that Public Debt has been increasing—and not decreasing—every year.

Everyone is all for more production, more competition and improved quality. But fact is that it was the erstwhile Government's 'Permit, License, Quota Raj' that hamstrung competition in both, Private and Public Sectors. Also it is good to remember that sections of the Private Sector have been understating production to escape excise, sales tax and income tax and even indulging in power theft. As for quality, foreign products excel mostly in packaging and presentation—and not in substance. Indian cereals, fruits, vegetables and meats taste better than imported stuff. Indian textiles are as good as any in the world.

We should certainly export goods for which there is a good market. But we don't have to be obsessed with exports. We must recognise that ours is a continental economy. (Out of a total of twenty-two climatic zones, we have twenty-one in India. Only we don't have Mediterranean climate, and so we can't grow olives.) That being so, we don't have to join the rat-race for exports. With every country trying to export more and more, we all can only end up *importing* more and more. Such a policy will profit importers and exporters, and shippers, bankers and insurers—and, incidentally, put a serious strain on our transport system—but it will not benefit the common man. Our primary objective must be to feed, clothe, house and educate our masses—and not maximise our foreign trade.

Bureaucratisation is no doubt the bane of India. It is particularly out of place in business enterprises. It is for the Government to see that it does not appoint retired IAS men as Chairmen and Managing Directors of PSUs. It can always recruit MDs etc., from the vast ranks of Business Executives.

It is true enough that many PSUs show losses and they have to be subsidised. But private enterprises can also fail; and Government subsidises them too. Also while PSUs don't cheat on excise, customs, income tax, many private enterprises do. On top of that some private parties cheat the Exchequer to the tune of billions of dollars by over-invoicing imports, and some others do it by under-invoicing of exports. Banks are showing lacs of crores of rupees as bad debts. The guilty parties here are private borrowers and not public borrowers.

Ever since we opened up our economy too much too fast, we have been suffering massive dumping, resulting in closure of many Indian enterprises and consequential unemployment. Even the Prime Minister conceded in February 2000, that the unemployment situation was 'appalling'. The Institute of Economic Growth of course felt that the situation was 'explosive'. Fortunately our family system can partly absorb the shock of unemployment. But otherwise the situation is serious.

As for making PSU shares available to the public, we can do so without handing over an entire PSU to a private company. Government could particularly make these shares available to labour.

This is not to suggest that there are no fit cases for privatisation. We all know of basket cases. There are cement factories in the public sector set up in places where there is no coal, no lime-stone, no water and not even a rail-head—just to please some local politician. And there are sick old cotton textile mills which are being prevented from dying a natural healthy death by artificial respiration of Government funds. The inefficiency of several nationalised banks has made it possible for foreign banks to set up shop in India and repatriate Rs. 1000 crores a year in foreign exchange as profits.

Government is not touching these their 'holy cows'; but it is planning to auction National Ratnas like Indian Airlines and Air India, BHEL, SAIL and ONGC. This is globalisation gone mad. It can only lead to foreign gobble-isation of Indian industry. Russia succumbed to this slogan and, in the process, sold its oil fields and other PSUs at one-third their real worth, and suffered a 50% decline in its GDP. We must learn from their harrowing experience. The Vajpayee Government is a popular government. It is pledged to the creed that 'India can, and shall, be built by Indians'. That

being so, it should give a second and closer look to this Disinvestment thing.

Public interest demands that:

(i) Government come out with a White Paper on the Disinvestment policy and performance during the last ten years.

(ii) Disinvestment should be decided not by one or more ministers but by a statutory Disinvestment Commission, representing experts and including labour;

(iii) The minimum reserve price of a PSU should be determined by market value or book value, *whichever is higher*. And here we should be guided by our own consultants and not by so-called foreign global consultants.

(v) In all cases of Disinvestment there should be a mandatory condition that the same shall *not* be sold to foreign companies.

We should not blindly follow IMF, World Bank or WTO but listen to the voice of reason and humanity as enunciated in Gandhiji's *Hind Swaraj*. Even Keynes, the greatest economist of the 20th century, has said: "I sympathise, therefore, with those who would minimise, rather than with those who would maximise, economic entanglements between nations."

Let people, mesmerized by the *mantra* of 'market', heed the words of George Soros, long-time apostle of capitalism: "Market fundamentalism is today a greater threat to open society than any totalitarian ideology....Global capitalism has allowed profit motive to penetrate non-economic fields of activity....(the result is) ideological imperialism....Market Fundamentalism seeks to abolish collective decision-making and impose the supremacy of market values over all political and social values."

Mankind is something more than the Market.

□

Foreign Invasion of Indian Insurance

American Insurance Companies are treated as financial lepers in USA.

—Time Magazine

In 1963—after the war with China—we were not in the best of shape. In that situation of weakness, the US pressed us to let it install a high-powered transmitter in India to be used during peak hours by the US and during lean hours by us. When this agreement became public there was a furore in the country. Pandit Nehru blamed the I & B secretary and quickly discarded the agreement.

This time too, under persistent Western pressure, New Delhi agreed to open the insurance sector to foreign business. But now though public opinion on the subject has expressed itself in no uncertain terms, will government correct its course?

If foreign insurance companies were good for India, we ourselves would have asked for them long ago. But the fact is that it is the foreign companies, backed by their respective governments, which have been insisting on invading our economy. Over the years, under Western pressure various governments were more than half inclined to open insurance to foreign behemoths. But they were afraid that nationalists and leftists would not let that happen.

Only four years back the then Finance Minister actually introduced the Insurance Regulatory Authority Bill in the Lok Sabha, opening insurance to the private sector and foreign sector. The BJP, even at that time was the largest party in the House. While a tiny group in the BJP Parliamentary party was willing to go along

with that Bill, the bulk of the members made it clear that while there was no objection to privatisation, 'foreignisation' (if I may coin that word) was not on. In this situation Mr. Chidambaram withdrew his bill to avoid defeat.

In the general election later that year the BJP manifesto reiterated its position when it said: "The broad agenda of the BJP will be guided by *Swadeshi* or economic nationalism." The National Agenda of the BJP & Alliance Partners also said: "We will continue with the reform process and give it a strong *Swadeshi* thrust to ensure that the national economy grows on the principle that 'India shall be built by Indians'." In this situation the Cabinet's sudden decision to open India to foreign insurance companies was out of character and uncalled for.

The LIC and GIC—are working well enough. For 1995-96, LIC had a total income (from premia and investments) of Rs. 22046 crores. GIC had a net premium of Rs 5,956 crores. During the last 15 years, LIC income has been growing at a healthy ten plus per cent a year—as against 6.7 per cent in the rest of Asia, 3.4 per cent in Europe and just 1.4 per cent in the US. (LIC has even provided insurance cover to 50 lakh people living below the poverty line with 50 per cent subsidy in the premium rates.) The LIC settlement of claims ratio at 95 per cent is also way above international averages. Even the GIC claims settlement of 74 per cent is way ahead of the international average of 40 per cent.

It could be argued that our insurance corporations could perform still better if there were competition. In that case, we can open insurance to Indian private enterprise. But why expose our insurance business to foreign assaults? The US has over 3,000 insurance companies. Most of them are incurring losses. And in recent years over 300 of them have gone bankrupt. The US Congressional Committee dealing with insurance, headed by Senator John de Dingell, has stated: "The annual yellow financial report filed by insurance companies with state commissioner is often called yellow peril because of its dubious reliability." *Time* magazine reports: "Like financial lepers, insurance firms have been widely shunned by most investors in the USA."

It is being touted about that foreign insurance companies will bring in foreign investment. They will not. If they have the money—and the mind—to invest, they can do so even now. And when they do invest, it will be our money, not their money. Meanwhile why do they have to infest our healthy insurance business on the doubtful promise of future investment?

The fact of the matter is that with their advertising blitz they will take away business from LIC and GIC, control Indian savings, and control even our pension and provident funds. They will give fancy salaries to the favoured few and, for the rest, replace men by machines. The American Insurance group with its capital base of $135 billion can easily afford to undercut losses for years till LIC and GIC are wiped out. At that stage, it can raise the premium rates and exploit its monopolistic position to bleed customers. Even their rating agencies like Standard & Poor and Moody will conspire with them to give them top ratings even in their year of collapse—as happened in the case of Enron.

But in the name of "free enterprise" they will refuse to invest in government securities and thus starve the Indian Government of funds for its social programmes (LIC invests 70 per cent of its funds with the Government). And then in the name of 'globalisation' they will take away thousands of crores in foreign exchange as 'profits'.

Already foreign banks operating only in big cities are taking away Rs. 1,000 crores a year as profits. India must require foreign banks to meet the social obligations that are being met by Indian banks—or get out. There must be a level playing field—and we cannot put foreign companies on a pedestal.

Every country protects its economy and its savings. In the US the insurance industry enjoys special protection. Germany and France have banned the import of foreign insurance for domestic risks. Switzerland has kept out foreign insurance companies totally. As Mr. Jose Ripoll, a former Deputy Chief of Insurance of UNCTAD says: "Open market for insurance business is a myth." The Asian tigers who opened up their economy too fast are today no more than little cats. Only India and China who decided to

hasten slowly in the matter are in a relatively better economic shape.

In the name of 'liberalisation' and 'globalisation' under the rubric of 'World Trade Organisation' (which is actually the West's Trade Organisation), the West is only trying to further penetrate Third World economies, firmly control Third World countries and perpetuate absolute Western domination of the world. That must not be allowed. For what is at stake is not just the insurance business. It is the future of India.

□

Industrial-Military Complex of USA

Corporations have been enthroned. An era of corruption in high places will follow.

—*Abraham Lincoln*
U.S. President

It is a Government of corporations, for corporations and by corporations.

—*Hayes*
U.S. President

The business of America is Business.

—*Hardinge*
U.S. President

The dollars we have sent abroad through Development Banks (as 'aid') come back home in increased exports and more U.S. jobs.

—*Lloyd Bentson*
U.S. Treasury Secretary

President Roosevelt and President Eisenhower of USA both complained of the Industrial-Military Complex ruling the roost in USA.

Sense and Nonsense of Patents

April 8, 1989 in Geneva was 'Black Saturday' for India.

—*Chitra Subramaniam*

Seven years ago when the then Government introduced Patent Amendment Bill in the Lok Sabha, the then Leader of the Opposition, Shri Vajpayee, had walked out in protest. In the Rajya Sabha, Congress had no majority. And the BJP's Opposition to the Bill compelled it to refer the same to a Select Committee of the House.

This time the BJP-led Government introduced the same Bill in the Rajya Sabha, with some minor changes.

The BJP did not oppose the Bill in 1995 because it had objection to any particular section or sub-section. It had objection to the whole philosophy of TRIPS (Trade-Related Intellectual Property Rights), worked out in the World Trade Organisation under GATT negotiations at Uruguay. And that objection remains.

The Indian Patent Act of 1970 gives patents for seven years. And while it gives process patents even for foods, drugs and chemicals, it does *not* give product patent for the same. As a result medicines—and medical treatment—are cheaper in India than almost anywhere else on earth. The mischief with TRIPS agreement is that it forces us to give product patent even for drugs and chemicals—and that too for twenty long years. All this can only lead to progressive increase in medical and other prices.

And thereby hangs a tale.

When Uruguay negotiations began, India took the logical line that since GATT (General Agreement for Trade and Tariffs) did not cover patents, the same could not be part of any world trade negotiations under GATT. However suddenly—and very mysteriously—our negotiators in Geneva gave up that strong position. Writes Chitra Subramaniam, ace investigative reporter, in her revealing *India is for sale*:

"India's departure from its principled position—that TRIPS cannot be negotiated under GATT—was so unexpected that for months after New Delhi had capitulated in Geneva on 8 April, 1989, developing countries were asking why. The day that agreement was reached was christened Black Saturday and a senior Latin American negotiator (who went on to become his country's Finance Minister) and a close friend of India, summed up the debacle with telling effect: 'It will take a long time for India and the rest of us to recover from this, if we can recover at all'." (p. 113)

Obviously, powerful forces were at work. The United States Trade Representative, Carla Hills, had asserted that she was prepared to "pry open developing country markets with a crow-bar" if she had to secure new markets for US companies. Carla Hills became Crow-bar Carla.

Now that the new Government has promised transparency, it could make the relevant file(s) on the subject public so that the country could know who took that suicidal decision—and why.

It is significant that three retired Chief Justices of the Supreme Court of India—Hidayatullah, Chandrachud and Shah—warned the country against the new patents regime. And yet the then Government in its wisdom went ahead with it!

It must be clearly understood that nobody is opposed to the 'First, Sole and True inventor' patenting his invention. Such persons are the salt of the earth. However, the all-time Greats of Science never even thought of patenting their inventions.Newton's inventions dawned on him in a 'trance'. Marconi saw 'Cosmic assistance' in his invention. Edison attributed his achievements to vehicle of a high source. Why, even more recent men of genius have not thought in terms of patents and money. Jagdish Chandra

Bose proved that plants have life. He also did significant work on wireless. But he did not go about patenting his inventions. An Afro-American Good Samaritan Mr. George Carver, found that peanuts are excellent food—Gandhiji had said they are as good as almonds—but nobody can eat them much. He, therefore, worked on peanuts and produced peanut butter which, today, is a billion-dollar business. But he did not do it for money; he did not take out any patent; he did it for the love of humanity. The inventing spirit follows his ideas not for gain, but driven by an inner compulsion which will not let him rest. That being so, even the expression "intellectual property" is offensive to good taste. Intellect is something much more than money or property.

In 1939 the US National Economic Committee took Ford's evidence on the subject. He was asked: "Would inventions be introduced if there were no patents?" And the great Edsel Ford replied: "I feel quite definitely, it would be carried on."

Knowing all this, there was a move in the 19th century—in the hey day of Free Trade—to abolish Patents altogether. Holland actually abolished them in 1869—and did not revive them, in sheer self-defence, until forty years later. It was the patent lawyers, with a vested interest in patent disputes, who killed that noble idea. Today literally lacs of frivolous patents—even dosage patents!—are being taken out every year. The two constants in patented drugs are attractive packaging and a generous dose of alcohol.

Today it is the Drug Lobby even more than the Gun Lobby that dominates the American scene. President Clinton was in trouble not because of Lewinsky affair; such affairs are as deplorable as they are routine in USA. But it was the Clintons' efforts to give USA an inexpensive medicare system that put them on the wrong side of the formidable Drug-and-Doctor Lobbies.

However, their drugs are as ineffective as their Lobby is powerful. It has been estimated that the contribution of modern medicine to US longevity in the last one hundred years is just eight per cent. The remaining 92 per cent improvement is due to chlorination of water, pasteurisation of milk, better handling of sewage and adequate proteins. But the Niagara of drugs continues

unabated, culminating of late in Viagra. However, what can even Viagra do for thirty per cent American males who have become incapable of procreation, thanks to American junk foods, junk drinks and junk drugs? Incidentally, American foods are not cooked, they are zapped or 'nuked'. All that these Viagra-users get is an illusion of potency. No wonder the *New York Times* has described it all as 'the poisoning of America'.

But meanwhile the redoubtable drug lobby marches on under the armour of patent law.

As Walton Hamilton, Professor of Law, Yale University, USA wrote in the *Foreign Affairs Quarterly* a few years ago: "The owner of a patent for a process by which food products are impregnated with a certain vitamin has created an ingenious patent structure. One concern is granted the right to its process in respect to raw breakfast foods, a second, in respect to cooked cereals; a third, food for horses, mules and asses; a fourth, food for cows used in the production of 'liquid milk' only; a fifth, food for cows whose milk is processed as surplus; and likewise through a succession of dogs, cats, wolves and white mice and so on down the gradations of the animal kingdom." (No wonder even cows in the West are going mad!) The learned Professor added: "In the application, the novelty is elaborated into a large number of claims; the language, forsaking alike simple English and good Science, becomes a polysyllabic and legalistic jargon....Enough is revealed to secure patent; but enough is held back so that an outsider cannot work the patent."

The improvement itself can be patented. So when an invention runs thin, numbers make up for a dearth of novelty through 'chain patent'.... The arsenal is as useful for offence as for defense; it puts the corporate owner in a position to say; "You cannot come into this industry, save by my leave." And now this flood will infest the Indian drug market!

Many thoughtful men in the West have said that developed countries are a big enough market for patented products and they need not charge patent fees from developing countries. Writes Prof. Edith Tilton Penrose of John Hopkins University, USA: "In

view of the general desirability of facilitating the economic development of 'backward' areas, it would be good policy to permit all non-industrial countries freely to use all foreign originated inventions in industries producing for the domestic market."

India could take up these and related issues at the time of the four reviews of the working of TRIPS in the next few years.

And meanwhile our Patent Office could also investigate the gross violation of our Patent Laws. Our HMT produces six million watches a year; but there are twenty million spurious 'HMT' watches in the Indian market! India produces just 9 million kgs of Darjeeling tea. But the world tea market registers 45 million kgs of Darjeeling tea! Patents are a racket.

□

The Trouble with U.S.A. ......

The trouble with this country is that you can't win an election without the oil bloc, and you can't govern with it.

—*F.D. Roosevelt*

No Society can survive, no civilization can survive, with 12-year olds having babies, with 15-year olds killing each other, with 17-year olds dying of AIDS, with 18-year olds getting Diplomas they can't read.

—*Gingrich*
Speaker, U.S. House of Representatives

America is a large friendly dog in a small room. Every time it wags its tail, it knocks down a chair.

—*Arnold Toynbee*

Importing Poisoned Foods

I care not much for a man's religion whose dog or cat are not the better for it.

—Abraham Lincoln

A few months back Government put 1429 items on Open General License. The reason given was that the earlier Government had signed the WTO. If we are to follow literally and mechanically all that the preceding Government(s) had pledged to do, why bother to change the Government? It is also said by way of explanation that while we have to remove all Quantitative Restrictions (QRs) as per WTO, we are free to raise customs duties on these items. Fact, however, is that customs duties have been repeatedly lowered all along the line—and rarely raised.

It is possible the Government has good enough reasons for removing QRs and lowering duties. However, these reasons have never been made public and subjected to public scrutiny. All that the people know is that imports are flooding the market, industries are closing down and unemployment is assuming, in the words of the Prime Minister himself, "alarming proportions".

A perusal of this new OGL list makes amusing reading. USA is now going to export to India, items like coconuts and *supari*, *paan* and *bidi*. Does USA grow these items—or will it pick them up cheap anywhere on earth—and then dump them in India?

However, thirty-nine other items make truly shocking reading. For these include carcasses and cuts and offal (rejected parts), fresh or chilled or frozen of cows, pigs, sheep, goats, turkeys, ducks,

geese, rabbits etc.

All American food items—including cereals, vegetables and fruits—are heavily chemicalised. (And chemicals must be presumed to be guilty, unless proved otherwise.) They grow big, fast and colourful; but they don't have the taste of natural crops. However, the way flesh foods are fabricated in USA is nothing short of criminal.

Centuries ago the Church in the West decided that animals have no souls. On top of this the US Animal Welfare Act specifically excludes animals, intended for slaughter, from its regulations. It costs just one cent to stun an animal, to spare it the pain of slaughter. But even that cent is 'saved' to increase profits. And when animals reach the slaughter-house, hungry and famished, they are not given any food because there is no time for this food to convert into flesh—and money. Abraham Lincoln, the great American President once said: "I care not much for a man's religion whose dog or cat are not the better for it." Judged by this criterion, USA is probably the most ungodly country on earth, though the dollar carries the legend, 'In God We Trust'.

Chicken are hatched and fattended in the same tight coop. They feel so miserable, they begin to poke each other with their beaks. And so they are do-beaked! Ninety per cent of these chicken suffer chicken cancer.

A normal sow delivers half a dozen piglets a year. But they are now medicated to produce twenty a year. And the new target is 45 piglets a year. The poor sow is artificially impregnated within two hours of its last delivery. Over eighty per cent pigs have pneumonia at slaughter time.

At the Animal Research Institute, they are trying to breed animals without legs—and chicken without feathers—again to minimise costs and maximise profits.

Bulls are castrated most painfully to produce 'steer' for their greater fat. More fat earns more money.

Since white meat fetches a higher price, calves are kept anaemic; and all iron-content is denied to them. Since in their hunger for iron, they lick iron bars, they are now being kept in wooden

stalls. In sheer desperation, these calves lick their own urine for traces of iron!

Through chemicals, these calves are made to put on 350 lbs. within six months. But they are so weak and anaemic that they will collapse and die if they were not slaughtered quickly. The sights, smells and sounds in these slaughter-houses are so horrible that there is a 43% turn-over of labour every month.

Cows are made to treble their milk yield. But their life span comes down from 20 years to four years. And on top of that, today no pesticide-free milk is available in the American market.

Factory-produced animals have thirty times the saturated fat of farm animals. And fat means more money; but it also means more disease!

All American foods are heavily chemicalised. And American meats have fourteen times as much pesticide in them as American plant foods.

When people partake of the flesh of these angry and unhappy animals, they imbibe all their misery. While this misery is not quantifiable, the chemicals that go into these factory flesh foods, are playing havoc with humans. Chemicals that hasten the growth of animals, go to hasten the premature physical maturation of children, who consume these animal meat. So boys and girls consuming these meats are maturing one to three years sooner. There is early menarche and late menopause for girls. There have been extreme cases of 5 year-young girls developing breasts—and growing pubic hair. In the sixties only half a per cent of U.S. college students were impotent. Today thirty per cent of them have a sperm count below 20 million which makes them incapable of procreation (*vide* The Shealy Institute, Springfield, Mo. 65803-4400, USA).

According to the Journal of American Medical Association, 97% of coronary occlusions are caused by this meat. And colon cancer, another big killer, is also a gift of these flesh foods.

Good old Gandhiji had said: "The greatness of a nation can be judged by the way its animals are treated." Government and people alike need to shun the poisoning of animal and man alike. □

IV. DEFENCE & DIPLOMACY

1. India's Great Military Tradition
2. India is at par with China
3. Some Questions to the US President
4. The Root Cause of Sept. 11, 2001
5. Why the World Loves & Hates America
6. Understanding the Muslim Mind

India's Great Military Tradition

India defeated Alexander.

—Marshal Zhukov

A recent seminar in New Delhi on 'India and China: Looking at each other' was a valuable effort at understanding the two countries and their respective civilizations. Particularly instructive was the discussion on 'Strategic Thinking in India and China in ancient times: Kautilya and Sun Zi'.

Expert opinion was that military thinking had been rather weak in India. Although Kautilya had written *Arthashastra*—a treatise on war, diplomacy, administration and empire—over 2,000 years ago, it was lost for ages and was rediscovered less than 100 years ago. On the other hand, Sun Zi's treatise on war—*Bingfa*—also written over 2,000 years ago, had all along been a living tradition in China. To this day the Chinese army proudly presents copies of *Bingfa* to visiting military leaders. And, believe it or not, *Arthashastra* is compulsory reading in the Pakistan Army. But the Indian military neglects both. Classical and Western military perception, therefore, is that India has no tradition of military thinking.

India suffered much more from Central Asian attacks than China. India was a much richer prize than China. Before invading India, Timur held a conference of his nobles to decide whether to attack India or China. They were all for going to India, despite difficulties like raging rivers, thick forests, brave soldiers and elephants—and not one of them preferred China—because of the temperate climate, the rich foods and fruits and the sheer wealth of India. All these attacks involved unprecedented destruction. It is, therefore, no surprise that much of the literature—from Buddhist scriptures to the *Arthashastra*—got lost. But tradition, whether military or any other, lives in the very blood of the people. Although the *Arthashastra*, as written tradition, was all but lost, it continued to live in the epics. The conventional wisdom is that Palmerston enunciated the wise adage: "There are no permanent friends and no permanent enemies; there are only permanent interests." However, Bhishma Pitamah said the same thing in the Shanti Parva of the *Mahabharata* 5,000 years ago!

It has been said that Mao Tse-tung followed Sun Zi when he went out and away on the Long March, to escape defeat. However, Krishna did the same thing; he fled, so that Mathura may be saved, which is why he is also known as *Ran-chhod* (the man who fled the field). Whether it is India or China, armies try to fight *Dharmayuddha*—ethical warfare—confining fighting to fixed hours in certain seasons, and not hitting below the belt. When, however, there is danger of losing a war, all armies resort—with varying degrees of success—to *Kuta-yuddha*, devious warfare, in which norms are given the go-by.

The British were telling us all the time that, by and large, we Indians were non-martial people, interested more in heaven than in earth. And their friends, the Americans, are telling us that we have no military tradition, and that we must not go in for modern arms. The idea, clearly, is to demoralise us and keep us weak. However, the entire Indian history has a very different message. It was Marshal Zhukov, the Russian hero of World War II, who told the Indian Military Academy, Dehra Dun, some 40 years ago, that India had stopped and defeated Alexander.

Although Western writers had boosted Alexander as "world conqueror", fact is that even regional kings like Porus in Punjab and Sabbas in Sindh had stopped him in his tracks. After that he did not dare to face Chandragupta. He, therefore, organised 'omens', to manufacture the excuse that the 'gods' did not want him to proceed any farther.

Alexander was followed by *Saka* (Scythian) invasions. But

Vikramaditya threw them out beyond Shikarpur (in Sindh) and Quetta (in Baluchistan). Today Indian history books wax eloquent about Ashoka but they are tongue-tied on Vikramaditya. The reason is obvious: Ashoka had turned non-violent and Vikramaditya had turned out the invaders. The British wanted us to remember Ashoka and forget Vikramaditya—so that we lay low, and did not rise against them.

Even before and after Chandragupta and Vikramaditya, Indians spread all the way from Central Asia to South-East Asia. They crossed mountains, deserts and seas to reach out to what Europe at the time described as Serindia (Chinese India) in Central Asia, and Indo-China in South East Asia. That this expansion had a military dimension is clear from the fact that the 14th century saw a titanic struggle between north and south Indo-China. The north, backed by the Chinese, prevailed over the south backed by Indians after a prolonged war because it had a shorter supply line and also because India had meanwhile been devastated by the Turks. That India should have been able to make this huge military effort 600 years ago speaks volumes for its military thinking and organisation.

Textbooks in India give the impression that beginning with Mohammed Bin Qasim, invaders just came, saw and conquered. The truth, however, is very different. According to Arab records, between 632 and 712 AD, the Arabs had made 14 attacks on Sindh; 13 of them were beaten back. It was only the 14th attack that succeeded. However, even after Mohammed Bin Qasim, Bapa Rawal of Mewar swept up to Punjab and went through Iran and Iraq. It is after him that Rawalpindi—the base city of the Pakistani capital, Islamabad—is named.

The Turkish Muslim invasion pulverised much of India. The wonder is not that we suffered much; the wonder, rather, is that we survived it. Soon enough, the attacking forces were Indianised. The Rajputs were coalition partners of the Mughal. India threw up mighty kings whose very titles, Jahangir (world-holder) and Shahjahan (ruler of the world), announced their reach as a superpower of the times. According to Abul Fazal, 400 years ago, India had a cavalry of 3,42,692 and an infantry of 40 lakh. What was the military thinking and organisation behind this vast force? And, what was the Indian component in Mughal military thinking? That is the matter to study.

All of north India was won for the British by the Bengal Army, composed mostly of Biharis. It was these Biharis who won the three Sikh wars. And yet because the Biharis rose in revolt in 1857, the British demobilised them, dubbed them 'non-martial' races and kept them out of the Army. To this day, Bihar continues to suffer from that persecution.

Today the tragicomic situation in India is that our history texts are Delhi-centric and king-oriented. There is no military history of India. What we need is a poly-centric history—that which will take note of Pune, Patna and Hampi no less than of Delhi and Agra—and a history that will be people-oriented and not royalty-oriented. Simultaneously we need to have a military history of India from the *Mahabharata* and *Ramayana* to 1857 and 1971. It is sad to note that post-1947 governments of India have consistently downgraded the military. While the military has to subserve the civil authority in a democracy, it must be given its due place of honour and importance. The politicians' fear of, and allergy to, the military, has to go. Let us not forget that every Indian god bears arms! □

'Scrap the Army'—Nehru

When India became free the Defence Chiefs prepared a Defence Policy Paper. Army Chief Gen. Lockhart sent it to Prime Minister Nehru for Government Directions on the subject. When Lockhart called on the Prime Minister he was almost thrown out. He told Maj-Gen. A.A. Rudra:

"The Prime Minister took one look at my paper and blew his top. 'Rubbish! Total rubbish! he shouted. We don't need a defence plan. Our policy is *Ahimsa* (non-violence). We foresee no military threats. Scrap the Army! The police are good enough to meet our security needs'."

—Gen. Rudra's Biography
by Gen. D.K. Palit

India is at par with China

There will be no peace until all nations are equally strong.

—Buddha

Some time back, Defence Minister George Fernandes said that China was our "potential threat number one". Subsequently the official spokesman and George himself partly recanted that statement. When Pokhran II materialised on May 11, many people felt that George had probably made that statement to provide the country with a rationale for it. He almost became popular on that score. However, bomb or no bomb, a statement like that was best not made at all. But the Chinese reaction to Pokhran crosses all limits.

Asking India to 'stop immediately' the development of nuclear weapons, Beijing made four points. One, that India's action reflected 'an outrageous contempt for the common will of the international community' in favour of the CTBT. Two, India is using the 'China threat' as an excuse for the development of its own nuclear weapons. Three, India is seeking 'hegemony' in South Asia. And four, 'the international community should adopt a common position in strongly demanding India to immediately stop its nuclear development programme.'

One wishes the Beijing friends had been more faithful to facts. With Russia, Britain and France opposing sanctions, and non-aligned nations and Arabs welcoming the Indian test, what is the 'international community' they are talking of? Regardless of whether 'China threat' is excuse or reality, the point is: If A-bomb is good for China, why is it not good for India? Or does Beijing think that the five old nuclear powers—which also hold the five permanent seats in the UN Security Council—must continue to lord it over the world? As for 'hegemony', India is by far the biggest and strongest country in South Asia. It is the predominant power in the entire Indian Ocean rim. That being so, why does it have to 'seek' any 'hegemony'?

As for the international community stopping India, one hopes by now Beijing has caught up with the fact that even the USA is not all that keen on sanctions. Former Secretary of State, Kissinger, former US National Security Adviser, Brzezinski and Speaker of US House of Representatives, Gingrich have come out against sanctions. Former chairman of the US Joint Chiefs of Staff and new Secretary of State, General Colin Powell, has actually said that the USA should "embrace India". Why, even President Clinton said that the US law on sanctions is unimaginative and inflexible and that he even has to 'fudge' facts to get round it.

Right now Beijing and official USA are busy wooing—and arming—Pakistan. They have been doing so for decades. And they are not likely to succeed any better now than they have before. On top of that the US is, if anything, even more unpopular in Pakistan than in India. Pakistan has known the US longer and closer.

If Beijing thinks it can keep India down by joining hands with the US, it is sadly mistaken. The US, as the leader of the West—which has dominated the Afro-Asian world for two hundred years—is very much interested in pitting one country against another, to maintain the global hegemony of the West. And within this overall scheme of things, it is more apprehensive of an expansionist China than of a resurgent India.

General Denis J. Reimer, Chief of Staff of the US Army, during his visit to India in 1998, projected China as a potential threat to the US in the next century. Delivering a lecture on "Downsizing the US Army", at the United Services Institute, New Delhi, General Reimer felt that in the coming years China would emerge from a regional competitor to a major competitor in

military terms to the US. He went on record saying that the US was watching China closely.

A few years back the *Los Angeles Times* published some world maps drawn by US official geographers, and gave an 'Analysis Forecast' (August 25, 1992) for the 21st century. One of these showed China losing Tibet, Sinkiang and Mongolia. It also showed North-East China (Manchuria) and the areas around Shanghai and Canton (Guangdong) becoming 'autonomous'. Obviously these are the lines along which the American strategic mind is working.

As a great civilization, China needs to think coolly and maturedly, and not position itself on the wrong side of India, another great civilization. An unfortunate factor in India-China relations since the end of World War II was Nehru's naive handling of these relations. At one stage when the Muslim League was demanding partition, he said that it was all a matter of will: If Muslims willed to be separate, nobody could keep them together. He added that, on the other hand, if India and China willed it, the two could come together and become one state. (Incidentally, did he aspire to preside over India and China from the heights of Lhasa?)

It is significant that the Chinese troops entered Tibet only after India had recognised the new regime in Beijing. In 1949, whatever little postal and police personnel were in Tibet, were all Indians. (From 1912 to 1950, there was not a single Chinese in all Tibet). However, instead of getting Tibet admitted to the UN, Nehru thoughtlessly conceded Chinese 'suzerainty' over Tibet. And the Chinese quietly interpreted 'suzerainty' as 'sovereignty', and gobbled up Tibet!

Notwithstanding Sardar Patel's advice to the contrary, Nehru did not even bother to get China to recognise the established border. Under this same naive leadership, India recognised the Chinese claim to Taiwan, without getting China to recognise the Indian rights in Kashmir. I am not saying this to reopen all these issues. But Beijing must realise that nothing is final in this world. In the last two centuries, there has not been a single decade when States' borders have not changed materially. If China can play games, so can India. And New Delhi may not be as naive in the next fifty years as it has been in the last fifty years.

That being so, China must think coolly, speak responsibly and act maturedly. It does not have to pretend that it belongs to the same league as the US—and that it is miles ahead of India. Only in the Fifties, Chou En-lai had candidly admitted in Delhi that India was far ahead of China. For decades, both India and China had about the same 3 per cent annual growth rate or GDP. Today China is reported to be well ahead of India. But this could change—and India could again get ahead of China.

In any case we don't have to take Chinese statistics too seriously. Twenty years back I found two official Chinese economists in Canton making contrary statements. So I asked them what precisely was the population of China. Their answer was revealing. They said: "For production purposes we are 900 million; for consumption purposes we are 1100 million." So much for Chinese statistics.

While in India the tendency is to play down production and income, in China the tendency is to exaggerate them. Chou En-lai actually pleaded for 'patriotic statistics'. A few years back Radio Beijing announced that China was producing more sweet potatos (*Shakarkandi*) than UK. The BBC was quick to report that Britain did not grow any sweet potatos. Nor is that all. China is reported to grow much more food than India. The fact, however, is that India counts only cereals as 'food' whereas China counts even its potato crop as food.

This is not to play down the great progress that China is reported to have made. But it must be clearly understood that in respect of resources—human, material and moral—India is as well placed as China, if not better. While China has much more territory than India, only 10 per cent of it is arable; the figure for India is 57 per cent. While India has 0.2 hectares of arable land per head, the figure for China is 0.08. The same is true for water resources; while India has 612 litres per head per year, China has 462 litres. China has more coal, but we have more iron. China has more oil but we have more Sun, rain and hydel potential. And we both have

huge and industrious populations. So basically the two countries are at par. That being so, China does not have to assume any airs.

We didn't go into a tantrum when China went nuclear; China does not have to go into a tantrum because India has gone nuclear. The two great countries have to think in civilizational terms. They have to recover from two centuries of foreign exploitation. To this end they have to help each other come up. They have to try understand each other's points of view. And they don't have to give each other any pinpricks.

When Buddha heard of Ajatshatru of Magadha attacking the Licchavi confederacy led by Vaishali, he was dismayed that his disciples of Magadha should have attacked his Sakya kinsmen. He sighed and said that perfect peace would never come until all the nations of the earth were equally mighty. Let India, China—and the US—all heed the sage counsel of the Enlightened One and not think and act petty.

□

U.S.A. against India-China Friendship

"You know it would be silly for the U.S. to favour a situation in which 800 million Chinese and 600 million people in this sub-continent form a group, that would be inconceivable. That would be a price that under no circumstances we would pay. About this, you should never have any doubts."

—*Kissinger to T.N. Kaul*
then Foreign Secretary of India, 1971.
(P.N. Dhar: Indira & The Emergency, p. 171)

On the eve of India-China war, 1962, "a large proportion of our Intelligence Bureau assessment was fed by C.I.A. and British Intelligence."

—*'War in High Himalaya'*
by Gen. D.K. Palit

Some Questions to the US President

American Intelligence Agencies have been playing games in India.

After almost a quarter century, the US President last year visited India. The Indian people welcomed him heartily. However, it is queer that the most talked of aspect of the visit was whether he would visit Pakistan also. When he decided to halt in Islamabad—but to halt there only briefly—he only half-pleased Pakistan and at the same time, half-displeased India. For the simple fact is that India-Pakistan relations are not very different from US-Cuba relations. And the question is: How would USA take an Indian President or Prime Minister visiting USA and Cuba on the same trip? We should do as we will be done by.

India is the world's largest democracy. And USA is the world's richest and strongest democracy. But the two maxi-democracies have not always been on the best of terms.

Independent India started off with very friendly feeling for USA. We remembered President Roosevelt's war-time solicitude for India's Independence. However, the international skies soon darkened with Cold War clouds. USA entered into a military alliance with Pakistan and sided with that State on the Kashmir issue. In sheer self-defence we sought—and got—USSR support. In this situation Mr. Nehru's Man Friday, Mr. Krishna Menon, no doubt contributed to avoidable irritations in Indo-American Relations. But, USA also further contributed to the same by persuading UK to detach Diego Garcia from Mauritius before

giving it Independence—and then setting up a military base on that island. And Diego Garcia is nearer to Chennai than Chennai is to Delhi! At the time of the Bangladesh Liberation War, USA openly tilted towards Pakistan and even moved its Navy from the Far East into the Bay of Bengal, in a bid to overawe India.

With the end of the Cold War it was expected that Indo-American Relations would be stabilised on an even keel. However, there have been quite a few hiccups on the way. USA sees itself as the sole super-power with interests all over the world and, after half a century of steady development, India views itself as not any the less important than four of the five "great powers".

The world today is a global village. This integration not only brings even remote countries together, it also highlights the differences between countries and communities suddenly thrown closer together. And these differences can be political, economic, military, social and cultural.

In the political realm the Kashmir issue has always soured Indo-American Relations. Two years back, when India initiated the Bus Diplomacy, USA was less than supportive. The CIA chief even went so far as to say that nothing would come of it. Soon after, USA acted very maturedly and condemned Pakistani armed intrusion into Kargil. However, it was noted that in the recent hijacking of an Indian plane, USA refrained from condemning obvious Pak involvement in that affair.

From time to time some US spokesmen have made very irresponsible statements. Ms. Jeane Kirkpatrick, then US ambassador at the UN, was reported as saying that "The break-up of India is one of the goals of American policy". *The Washington Times*, a paper known to be close to CIA, foresaw on March 1, 1991 "The break-up of such states as Yugoslavia and India". On March 14, 1991, *The Telegraph* of Calcutta reported the General Dynamics, top US arms suppliers, telling defence experts in Washington that the US war machine could be used to 'neutralise' India.

US intelligence agencies have also been playing games in India. In 1984, Air India plane 'Kanishka' blew up over the Atlantic. Later it was established that the saboteurs had their

training in a sabotage school run by FBI agents. In December 1995, lethal arms were air-dropped in Purulia. Indian Intelligence agencies found out that it was a CIA operation—and that CIA had not informed even ISI about it though this plane took off from Karachi. CIA and FBI play games even in USA, which is bad enough. But playing such games on the international chess-board can embitter feelings and derail international relations.

Indo-American Relations in the economic field are also less than happy. We know that, as US President Coolidge put it, "The business of America is business." But many in the developing world have a feeling that the GATT negotiations culminating in WTO, crossed the limits of legitimate business. It was under American pressure that the Rajiv and Rao Governments agreed to amend the excellent Indian Patent Law. TRIMS and TRIPS also went beyond the proper scope of GATT, which covered only trade and tariffs. US negotiator Carla Hills went so far as to say that she would "Pry open developing country markets with a crow-bar". Under US-WTO pressure, India has put thousands of consumer items on OGL and drastically cut customs duties. This has hurt many Indian industries and thrown countless people out of jobs.

While health-conscious Americans are giving up smoking, US Government is helping American cigarette majors to invade India, China, Japan, Russia and other countries. WTO's Codex Alimantarines Commission permits DDT residue in the developing world 50 times that in the US! Even the US agricultural Secretary Yeutter, under President Bush Sr., said that "WHO will defeat health laws". But USA is permitting damage to Afro-Asian health, just to promote American business interests.

It is a matter of satisfaction that thinking Americans are raising their voice against market fundamentalism which is spreading its wings in the booming name of 'globalisation'. As David C. Korten writes in his *When Corporations Rule the World*: "Economists know the price of everything and the value of nothing." Globalisation is about profits; Governments are about people. The USA needs to listen to the voice of people all over the world and not only to its business lobbies, if it is to command

any moral authority in the world.

In the military realm also Indian and American perceptions vary widely. The world cannot be frozen in the 1945 mould which recognised only USA, UK, France, USSR and China as 'Great Powers'. If nuclear arms and missiles are good for some powers they cannot be presumed to be bad for other powers. It was therefore churlish for USA to deny us super computers and press even Russia, not to sell cryogenic engines to India. These are instruments for advancing to the frontiers of science and technology and the USA should not be seen as obstructing India from coming into its own.

The cultural dimension of Indo-American Relations is, if anything, even more important. A couple of years back an American owned TV channel rubbished Mahatma Gandhi himself. It was condemned on the floor of Indian Parliament as 'cultural terrorism'. Later when Pepsi wanted to boost its sales, it called Michael Jackson and not any Indian artistes. More recently, India found itself invaded by 'Valentine Day'. Now love is as old as life. And we in India not only have a regular God of Love (Kama), we have even produced *Kama Sutra*, a classic on the art and science of love. But, an institution like 'Valentine Day', with no roots in Indian life and culture, can only annoy Indian society.

India notes with satisfaction American interest in Indian thought and Indian practices like *Yoga* and meditation and herbal medicine etc. And USA is a big multi-purpose magnet not only for many in India but for many in the world. Let these cultural forces interact and produce a variety of synthesis. But let these not be prodded by big bucks or big guns.

These are the problems; and no Presidential or Prime Ministerial visits can solve them. But high-profile visits like these are an appropriate occasion for massive feed-backs to the countries engaged in such diverse converse. And let that provide a solid basis for fair and fruitful cooperation in the years and decades to come. □

The Root Cause of Sept. 11, 2001

CIA was interpreted to Indonesians as 'Chinese Intelligence Agency'!

What happened in New York and Washington on Sept. 11, 2001, has amazed and stunned the world. Why were the Arabs so angry as to do what they have done? And are they the only ones to resent USA? The story goes back to at least 1945, the closing days of World War II.

Truth about Hiroshima: The American explanation for atom-bombing Hiroshima and Nagasaki was that otherwise it would have taken five lakh American lives to defeat Japan. *This is not true.* Weeks before Hiroshima, Tokyo was burning. In a single night raid, one lakh and eighty thousand people had been roasted alive by napalm in Tokyo. Japan, therefore, had offered to surrender. But this offer was not accepted quickly. Hiroshima was atom-bombed to over-awe the world, and do, probably, certain other things e.g. about Subhas Bose. (Had Bose not died in mysterious circumstances, he, and not Nehru, would have become Prime Minister, and there would have been no partition of India).

The Bogus Cold War: Soon after World War II ended, the West launched its Cold War. World War II had reduced USSR to shambles. It was no threat to anybody. But the end of war would have led to economic depression. USA wisely decided on Marshal Plan to rebuild Western Europe and, incidentally, earned its gratitude. But there is no business like Arms trade. (Even the Pope invests Vatican money in American arms industries). And so the

Cold War was launched to have an excuse for re-arming in a big way. As a result we got the Korean War and the Vietnam War.

The Korean Trap: The US President Truman had said in February 1950 that USA was not interested in Korea and that it was withdrawing its forces from that country. The Truman announcement was viewed as an invitation to re-unite North and South Korea, which had been divided by USA and USSR against the wishes of Koreans. But as soon as North Korea moved in, USA got the UN to declare it aggressor. It was a case of entrapment. (USSR could not use its veto in the Security Council because it was unwisely boycotting UN at the time, for not letting China take its seat in that organisation!) At one stage US Commander MacArthur even wanted to atom-bomb North Korea. It was probably Attlee's warning dash to Washington that averted the tragedy. Incidentally, to this day, USA does not like North Korea and South Korea becoming even friends!

Vietnam War: USA had no business to go and fight the Vietnamese and cause them and itself great havoc.

Genocide in Indonesia: In Indonesia, Soekarno was toppled and a few lakh leftists murdered. People heard it was a CIA operation. Americans cleverly interpreted 'CIA' as 'Chinese Intelligence Agency.' And Indonesians, who resent the high Chinese position in that country, believed that story!

Truth about Afghanistan: For decades, Afghanistan had been closer to USSR than to USA. USA's friend, the Shah of Iran, tempted Daud, Prime Minister of Afghanistan, to forget about USSR and get close to USA. Communists in Afghanistan didn't like it. One of their top leaders was murdered. In this situation the Reds took over the Government. When Iran took 144 American hostages, Russia thought USA would not take that lying down and would occupy Iran and thus threaten the Western flank of their protege. (Incidentally, Reagan, Kissinger and other Republican aspirants for office privately persuaded Iran *not* to release the hostages just then, since that would go to the credit of President Carter, and help his re-election!) However, the Russians had proved wrong. USA did not go to Iran. But meanwhile USSR got trapped in Afghanistan, with Pakistan, USA and Saudi Arabia backing the

Afghan Opposition. They also helped create the Taliban. The rest, as they say, is history.

Iran-Iraq War: USA has also been playing games in the Persian Gulf area. Kuwait was carved out after World War I just to deny Iraq a sea opening. Iran and Iraq are divided by Shatt-ul-Arab estuary. Normally in such situations, the mid-stream is considered the border. But in this case, when the Shah of Iran was friend of USA, Iraq was forced to concede the whole breadth of the stream to Iran. But when Iran went 'Islamic', Iraq was encouraged by USA to ask for midstream as the border! When Iran demurred, Iraq was encouraged to attack Iran. When Iran more than stood its ground, and even unwisely rejected multibillion dollar compensation offered by Saudi Arabia—Americans shot down an Iranian civilian plane, to warn and force Iran to ceasefire.

The Kuwait Trap: The USA wanted to station its troops in West Asia to police that area for good. The Iraq-Kuwait issue came handy here. Kuwait was pumping out oil too close to the Iraqi border—and thus depleting the Iraqi oil wells. Iraq was furious. The US envoy in Iraq, and later its Under Secretary of State, told Saddam on two different occasions: "We know you have problems with Kuwait but we are not interested." Saddam took this as American permission to get even with Kuwait. However, the moment Iraq went into Kuwait, the US accused it of aggression. When some diplomats said that now that USA had asked Saddam to withdraw, he would do so, the Secretary of State told them, "We have taken all steps to see that he does *not* go back". The result was a murderous war—and no less murderous sanctions—causing the death of half a million Iraqi children. But the Iraq-Kuwait War enabled USA to station troops in nearby Saudi Arabia, the keeper of Islamic holies in Mecca and Medina, which irritates Muslims all over the world.

Palestine: The way USA has consistently sided with Israelis against Palestinians, is a standing grievance with Arabs.

Punishing Osama Bin Laden or Taliban or Afghanistan, or anybody else, is not going to solve the problem that erupted on September 11. Only a serious re-thinking of American Foreign Policy in all its dimensions can hope to tackle that problem.

□

Why the World Loves & Hates America

The world sees menace in American Values.

—New York Times

The titanic tragedy of September 11 has changed the world for good. Old assumptions, old expectations, old attitudes, old equations are no longer valid. One wishes September 11 had not happened at all. Or if the hijackers were so aggrieved that they had to do it and shock the world, they could have at least done it on a week-end, destroying the towers but sparing the thousands of innocent lives.

The West, led by the USA, has given the world much science and technology, wealth and welfare, democracy and opportunity. And this attracts millions of promising young persons from all over the world. But all this achievement has a seamy side. However, such is the power, the wealth, the weaponry and self righteousness of the US establishment, Americans have come to believe that they alone, and always are right. Even forgetting the genocide of Red Indians in the 18th century and a murderous Civil War in the 19th century USA indulged in excesses even in the 20th century. They atom-bombed Hiroshima and Nagasaki and made war in Korea and Vietnam.

Countries were invaded, Governments toppled, and elected leaders thrown out and even murdered, with reckless abandon. In Palestine the UN Partition plan was forgotten and Israelis were favoured at the cost of Palestinians.

The recent Afghan and Kuwait Wars were particularly cynical.

USA has dominated the world economy for decades. But not content with that, it converted GATT (General Agreement for Trade & Tariffs) into WTO (World Trade Organisation). And the world finds that WTO is only the West's very own Trade Organisation. It has forced countries to change their patent laws to American satisfaction. And it has forced them to let in foreign insurance companies. With tobacco sales falling in USA, America is forcing its cigarettes on the world. US companies have genetically altered seeds and even come up with Terminator Seeds. It is a direct assault on the food security of nations. On top of this US negotiator Carla Hills threatened to break open the markets of developing countries, with a 'crow bar'.

On issue after issue, USA has defied the world. It refuses to curb the free sale of small arms. It refuses to ban land mines. It has gone back on the Kyoto Pact to control pollution. It does not want an International Criminal Court to prosecute war crimes, genocide and crimes against humanity. For years it had not paid some $ 1 billion in UN fee arrears. The UN hit back last summer by electing Libya and Algeria, but not USA, to its Human Rights Commission! After September 11 it hurriedly paid about half the arrears—but still not any interest on late payment.

The USA is equally isolated on Germ Warfare issue. It has secretly built a germ factory in Nevada that could wipe out whole cities, in violation of the Global Treaty banning such weapons. Crippled children in Vietnam are a creeping proof of American use of poison gas (Agent Orange) in the Vietnam War. And the 'depleted uranium' used in munitions by USA in Iraq has killed not only Iraqis but even US soldiers by cancer.

Under business pressures, USA permits excessive use of chemicals in agriculture and flesh foods. Most Americans, reported the *Washington Post* (23.3.2001) "carry traces of deadly toxins". Recently President Bush said, "As you know we're studying safe levels for arsenic in drinking water." Asked the *New York Times* (2.4.2001): "What has America done to deserve

the Arsenic President? "

As a result of chemicalised foods, there have been cases of five-year young girls developing breasts and pubic hair (John Robbins: *Diet for a New America*). Forty years ago only 0.5% college students in USA were sterile; today they are thirty per cent. (Norman Shealy: *Miracles Do happen.*) No wonder USA has developed 'Viagra'. Leading TV evangelists Jerry Falwell and Pat Robertson said on September 14 that USA deserved September 11. Divorce, homosexuality, abortion etc., in USA, they said, had driven "God mad". 'God', they said, "will not be mocked."

Thanks to the power of big business and the purblindness of the all-powerful media, most of these facts are hidden from most people. But the impact of American culture is sweeping the youth in many countries off their feet and disturbing well-established societies to their dismay.

Russia is surprised by a sea of advertisements blotting out Historic Vistas. China is surprised by youngsters naming themselves 'Fish', 'Magic', 'Medusa', 'Satan'. Japanese teenagers have become rude. "It has come to the point that teaching polite language to Japanese is like teaching a foreign language" said the *Yomiuri* weekly magazine.

USA's Time Warner has become 'the Leading Cultural Polluter', with its Geto Boys lyrically singing about 'slitting women's throats and cutting off their breasts.' No wonder the *New York Times* said: "The World sees a menace in American Values" (10.4.2000).

Particularly serious is the American assualt on Hindu and Muslim religions and traditions. In the last two years McDonald and some other American MNCs have run down Diwali fire-crackers and boosted an alien Valentine Day. Waleed Al-tabtabaie, a leading Kuwait M.P., has condemned the organising of Valentine Day in Muslim countries as violative of Muslim morals. Sending Christian missionaries with foreign money to proselytise people behind the smoke-screen of schools and hospitals is as dishonest as it is offensive. For as Gandhiji put it "It is not unusual to find Christianity synonymous with denationalisation."

All these negative aspects of American life did not begin with President Bush. But many of them have grown worse during his presidency. Mr. Jervis, Professor of International Politics at Columbia University, has said that much of the world sees "the prime rogue state today is the United States". And Maureen Dowd of *NYT* has said: "Doesn't Bush realize that EVERYBODY in the world HATES America?"

Although September 11 and Bush's sturdy response to it has improved his ratings, apprehensions persist even in Europe. *Der Speigel*, leading German weekly, recently denounced the arrogance of USA as 'snarling ugly Americans'. And the French Prime Minister said USA is not a super-power, it is only a hyper-power. *Le Monde* said: "The allies are offering military means to the Americans and they're using them like a super-market according to their needs." And the German *Sueddeutsche Zeitung* wrote: "America, the world power, has rediscovered the UN system these days, but is following the raisin-in-the-cake theory of picking out what looks good and tossing most of the rest aside." It wants money from everybody but soldiers only from Britain.

It is about time USA took note of Gorbachev's advice to the US President: "Mr. Bush, the World Doesn't Want to Be American" (*Washington Post*, 1.1.2001), and realised: "The World is complicated, it contains and expresses a variety of interests and cultures. Sooner or later, International Policy including that of the United States, will have to come to terms with that variety."

Out of the September 11 evil may yet come some good.

□

Corporations Above The Law

Corporations have neither bodies to be punished, nor souls to be condemned; they, therefore, do as they like.

—*Lord Thurlow*

Understanding the Muslim Mind

What Muslims need is a Reformation and a Renaissance.

What happened in New York and Washington on September 11, 2001 has shocked the world as it has not been shocked before in living memory. USA is very very angry. And it has every reason to be all that angry. More than the grievous injury, it is the gross insult of it all that has hurt USA. However, fundamentalism and terrorism did not begin with Osama; and they are not likely to end with him.

1757 marked the beginning of Western domination of the World at Plassey. 1857 confirmed that domination—but it also made it clear that domination could not go on forever. 1947 marked the beginning of the end of Western physical domination. And 2001 confirms that end—with the promise of a new and balanced world order. Such is the cycle of history.

Apart from 1857, India showed its resentment against the West in 1905 and 1921. China showed its resentment in the Boxer Revolt of 1900, and the Communist revolution of 1949. And the Muslim world has been showing its resentment since World War I. In the context of September 11 the world particularly needs to understand the Muslim mind.

After Buddha, Vikrama and Shankara in India, Kung Fu-tse, Shih Huang Ti and Lao-tzu in China, and Plato, Socrates and Aristotle in Greece, it was Islam that dominated much of the world in the Middle Ages. Three hundred years ago, the three biggest empires in the world, based in India, Persia and Turkey, were all Muslim. Even China and Russia were ruled by the Mongol Khans. Before King John of England signed the Magna Carta with his recalcitrant nobles, he had sought the support of the Sultan of Morocco, and even offered to embrace Islam in the bargain. Only two hundred years ago Napoleon toyed with the idea of embracing Islam, in an effort to control West Asia. He even asked what he and his soldiers of the Grand Army would need to do to become Muslims. He was told they would have to undergo circumcision; and he had no objection to that. But he was also told that they would have to give up wine; and no Frenchman would even think of it. That was the power and reach of Islam until modern times. But when Muslims remember that, and see their present conditions, they feel scandalised. Their feelings are aptly expressed in Iqbal's *Shikwa* and Hali's *Mussadas* in India.

Lots of people all over the world have the feeling that Islam is intolerant and violent. And this is true enough. The concepts of *kafir* and *jehad* are wholly unacceptable. Unfortunately this intolerance is the common heritage of all the three Semitic religions—Judaism, Islam and Christianity.

The misfortune of Islam is that it has had no Reformation, no Renaissance. This situation, said Sri Aurobindo, needs to be corrected: "We must strive to remove the causes of misunderstanding by mutual knowledge and sympathy and spread juster views of Mohammedan history and civilization. What is wanted is some new religious movement among the Mohammedans which would remodel their religion and change the stamp of their temperament." (*Karmayogin*, Vol. 2, p. 24)

The Prophet of Islam has been demonised by many. Dante put him in the lowest depths of hell. But Carlyle thought him the greatest of prophet-heroes, though he later apologised for it. The fact is that he was a reformer of his society, father of Arab nationalism and founder of almost a millennium-long Pax Islamica.

Islamic Allah is *Rab-ul-Aalimeen* (God of all mankind) and not *Rab-ul-Muslimeen* (God of Muslims only). The *Koran* says: "Noblest religion is this—that others may feel safe from thee. The

noblest Islam is this—that all may feel safe from thy tongue and hands." He said that in seeking knowledge one may go even as far as China. And he said he got cool breezes from India. It is the invaders who, by their excesses, got a bad name for Islam.

Mohammed was a business executive. And so the *Koran* is full of trade terms. Apart from the sword and fire of the conqueror, Muslim armies also carried goods and services, culture and civilization. There were regular trading *caravans* from Banaras to Baghdad. It was the Arabs who crossed Gibraltar, occupied Spain and carried crop rotation and other scientific agricultural practices to the then Spanish province of Holland. From Holland these practices went to England. The result was an Agricultural Revolution, which, in turn, helped trigger the Industrial Revolution in England, with financial help from India. Such is the varied history of Islam.

The West has given the world science and technology. It has also introduced the concept of democracy and human rights. But it has also rubbished India, China and the Muslim world. It has imposed itself on these civilizations. Missionaries have been sent with foreign funds to subvert the religion and culture of these people. Muslims resent it more because they have recent memories of their power.

Many Muslim countries were occupied. Even after 'Independence', their governments are either toppled or turned into puppets. Their oil wealth goes to enrich the West. Their oil revenues are diverted to arms purchases. Neighbouring countries are encouraged and armed—to fight each other. According to Paul Kennedy, there is an annual flow of over $ 40 billion from the poor countries to the rich countries (*Preparing for the Twenty-first Century*, *P. 224*).

In Iran when Mossadeq's popular Government nationalised oil, they toppled him. So much money was distributed as bribes that Nehru told the Indian Parliament that the value of the dollar fell in Teheran *bazaar*. In Egypt when Nasser nationalised the Suez Canal, UK, France and Israel invaded that country. When Algeria was poised to give itself a nationalist government, they stopped

and cancelled the elections mid-way and had military rule imposed on the country. In Pakistan they installed a series of Generals. Taliban is CIA and ISI gift to Afghanistan. Perhaps the worst insult to Afro-Asia is the West's media manipulation. They devote the greatest attention to the Third World in times of disaster, crisis and confrontation. If there is a famine or earthquake they will arrive, only to say that food and other assistance is not being distributed fairly. CNN showed how an American missile can be pin-pointed through a ventilator in the war against Iraq—just to overawe the world. During the Cuban missile crisis in 1961, the Western media said Khrushchov had yielded to Kennedy and agreed to withdraw those missiles. They almost suppressed the fact that, in return, USA had agreed to withdraw its missiles from Turkey, aimed at Russia!

The West has given much to the world. So has every civilization in its day. Old wrongs have to be righted and a New and Fair World Order established. The vital interests and cultures of nations have to be protected. They cannot be smothered by the 'sole super-power' in the booming name of 'globalisation'. If the world now begins to move in this direction, the martyrs of World Trade Centre and Pentagon will not have died in vain.

□

U.S. paying for past mistakes: Clinton

Washington, Nov. 9—The former U.S. President, Mr. Bill Clinton, has said terror has existed in America for hundreds of years and that the nation is "paying a price today" for its past mistakes.

The former U.S. President, who received a warm welcome from a 1000-strong audience at his Alma Mater Georgetown University yesterday, said: "Here in the United States, we were founded as a nation that practised slavery." "This country once looked the other way when a significant number of Native Americans were dispossessed and killed to get their land or their mineral rights or because they were thought of as less than fully human. And we are still paying a price today," he said.

V. INDIA & PAKISTAN

1. Karachi Demolishes Two-Nation Theory
2. Sindhis and Mohajirs Look to India
3. India, Pakistan and the Bomb
4. Some Lessons of Agra

Karachi Demolishes Two-Nation Theory

We are also persons of Indian origin.

—Mohajirs in Pakistan

For several years now, Karachi has been on the boil. There are hundreds of killings every year. The thing to note is that these are not Hindu-Muslim killings: they are Muslim-Muslim killings. And they are taking place in the first city of Pakistan. Indeed the situation is so serious that the former Prime Minister, Mr. Nawaz Sharief asked then Prime Minister, Ms. Benazir Bhutto to "save Karachi first and then talk of Kashmir". Ms Bhutto in turn has been asking the Mohajir Qaumi Mahaz (National Front of Refugees) leader, Mr. Altaf Hussain to condemn Indian 'atrocities' in Kashmir and not to compare Karachi with Kashmir. But Altaf Hussain is clear that things are far worse in Karachi than they are in Kashmir or even Bosnia. He has also appealed to Muslims in India to protest against the genocide of Mohajirs—migrants from India—in Pakistan and to pray for their security and welfare.

Although the migrant-local problem has erupted in Pakistan only in the last 10 years, it has been simmering from day one of Partition. While refugees from East Punjab were accommodated in West Punjab, those from Delhi, U.P., Bihar etc., were told to go south, to Sindh. Shaukat Hayat Khan, the son of Sir Sikandar, long-time Premier of Punjab, used to meet all trains arriving in Lahore from India and tell non-Punjabi migrants: *Pakistan aur aage hai* (Pakistan is farther ahead). Thus, these refugees landed up in Sindh.

In the first flush of Islamic zeal, these refugees were welcomed into Sindh but within weeks the Sindhis realised that they had not bargained for such a situation.

Pre-partition Sindh had a population of 40 lakh, 30 per cent of which was Hindu. While about 10 lakh Hindus came away, the refugees from India were many times that number, and today they claim to be over two crore. Sindh could not but explode in such a situation.

Sindhi Muslims had opted for Partition like Muslims elsewhere in the country. Not many of them expected Pakistan, but it sounded good to talk big. In the unlikely event of Partition, mass migration was not visualised but Sindhi Muslims hoped somehow to help themselves to Hindu property. As it happened, Partition did come about and there was mass migration to and fro, but lands and houses left behind were declared evacuee property. Hindu property went to refugees or Mohajirs; the Sindhi Muslims felt cheated.

More importantly, though there had been Hindu-Muslim tension in Sindh, it had not been bitter. The Sindhis shared the Sufi tradition and sang Shah Abdul Latif's *Sufi Kalaam*. The Sindhi Muslim was not prepared to see the Mohajir replace his Hindu neighbour. The 'devil' one knew was better than the devil one didn't.

The Sindhi Muslims viewed the mass migration as *Qiamat* (the Hindu *Pralaya*). Within days, Jinnah's portraits were removed from shops. The Mohajirs' language was ridiculed as 'Urdu-Phurdu'. They were described as 'Red Mouths' on account of their fondness for *paan*. Sindhi Muslims refused to join in killing the Hindus; as a result less than 1,000 Hindus were killed in Sindh in 1947-48. The Muslim refugees were so angry with the 'non-cooperation' of local Muslims, that they started to say: "How is a Sindhi Muslim born? From the urine of Hindus."

The Sindhi points out that Muslims totalled 13 per cent in U.P. but they had 45 per cent of the jobs. He remains unimpressed by the Mohajir justification for coming away: that there were riots, because he reasoned that if millions of Muslims could live in India, why couldn't the Mohajirs?

The Sindhi is shocked to see all the major cities of Sindh—

Karachi, Hyderabad, Sukkur—taken over by non-Sindhis. He finds himself a stranger in his own land. He keeps asking: "Even the British officers appointed to serve in Sindh were required to learn Sindhi. Why don't the Mohajirs learn Sindhi?" And the Mohajirs' feeling is: "We came here for Islam; we did not come here to become Sindhis."

The Sindhi is right, but the Mohajir is not wrong either. And matters are further complicated by the scarcity of resources. Pakistan spends 80 per cent of its budget on defence and debt servicing. That leaves pretty little for health, education, roads. The result is an all-round feeling of deprivation.

The Mohajirs claim that they account for at least half the population of Sindh. The 1991 census showed that 80 per cent was Sindhi and 20 per cent was Mohajir. These census figures were rejected by the government of Pakistan as doctored by Sindhi enumerators. The Mohajirs point out that while they account for 50 per cent of the population of Sindh, only one per cent of the Sindh police is Mohajir. Although they are 20 per cent of the population of Pakistan, "Urban Sindh" that is the Mohajirs, get only 7.6 per cent of available college admissions and services recruitment. Of 71,000 top jobs available in Pakistan the Mohajirs say they hold only 178. A Sindhi Muslim educationist, who happened to be my classmate at college, told me that as most Mohajirs had an urban background they made better students. But Sindhis see themselves as "sons of the soil" and they also invoke the OBC argument. As a result, jobs are not given on the basis of merit. India and Pakistan have the same kind of problems.

Since India was partitioned on the basis of the two-nation theory, the Mohajirs want to know why three lakh Biharis are rotting in Red Cross camps in Bangladesh and not allowed to enter Pakistan. (Liaqat Ali had said Sindh could accommodate all Indian Muslims). In 1951, Indian Muslims were stopped from entering Pakistan; in 1961, Indian Muslim doctors and engineers were barred from applying for jobs in Pakistan. The two-nation theory, says Mr. Altaf Hussain of the MQM, has been reduced to a joke.

The MQM demands a fair share of power in Sindh and Pakistan. For, as Mr. Hussain puts it, people in Pakistan do not see

themselves as Pakistanis but as Sindhis, Punjabis, Pathans and Baluchis. The Mohajirs, he says, are the fifth nationality.

The Mohajirs were the most enthusiastic of all Pakistanis but they are beginning to recognise their Indian roots. Way back in 1948, a tailor from Jaipur had told me in Hyderabad Sindh, that "the water of Jaipur is like ghee." When India took in "persons of Indian origin" from Idi Amin's Uganda, the Mohajirs said, "We are also persons of Indian origin; why does not India take care of us?" some Mohajirs are writing Hindi poetry; Hindi, they say, has a certain "earth-coolness" (*sheetalta*) about it. Some of them are devotees of Satya Sai Baba. Some now recollect that they come from the land of Buddha, Krishna and Kabir. Fortunately, of late Sindhis and Mohajirs have come closer. MQM leader Altaf Hussain describes Mohajirs as Urdu-speaking Sindhis. Recently he married a Sindhi lady, Miss Gabol. He has described Partition as the "biggest folly in History" and he sang: *Sare Jahan se achchha, Hindustan hamara.*

□

Indus unites India, Pakistan

Many Pakistani scholars and writers, in their zeal to justify partition and without seeking the primordial roots of the process, yet with a passion for eschewing all that was Indian, chose to trace their country's cultural foundations solely to extra-territorial linkages. In denying the Indian, they denied the Indus...

Indra and the Vedas, Krishna and the Mahabharata are to be shunned as if they would pollute the minds of the youth; as if Islamic faith is itself vulnerable to such influences with which it has co-existed for centuries and not been overcome. Yet these deities and beliefs are facts forming a part of Indus history....Without comprehending these, it may never be possible to understand the justifiable pride that a very important section of present-day Indus society, the Mohajir, takes in its association with his birthplaces in Agra, Lucknow and Allahabad.

—*Aitzaz Ahsan*
(The Indus Saga)

Sindhis and Mohajirs Look to India

Does India have a role in Pakistan? No—and Yes!

In 1983, when the Movement for the Restoration of Democracy in Pakistan launched its agitation, some 500 Sindhis laid down their lives. Scores of Sindhis have since died fighting for democracy. Earlier there were reports that dacoits were looting buses and trucks plying on the national highways in Sindh and creating lawlessness in the countryside. Many Pakistani leaders are beginning to wonder if Sindh is going the Bangladesh way.

How and why has Sindh set out on a separatist course? In the first place it should be remembered that the Pakistan movement was really strong only in areas where the Muslims were in a minority and therefore, felt unsure. In the January 1946 elections, although Sindh had a 71 per cent Muslim population, for every four Muslim votes cast for the Muslim League, three Muslim votes were cast for the nationalist Muslims led by Mr. G.M. Syed and Maula Bux. The Sindhi Muslim support for Pakistan was quite ephemeral. Since the Hindus opposed it, the Muslims thought it must be good for them. They also thought that if Partition led to the exit of Hindus, they would get the properties left behind. However, the arrival of Bihari Muslim refugees in Sindh even before August 15, 1947, changed all that. Hindu assets were declared evacuee property, and later handed over to the refugees from India.

Nor was that all. Before Partition, Muslims in Sindh were

demanding a 70 per cent job reservation, but after the Hindus departed and Muslim refugees filled the void, Sindhi Muslims felt cheated. The first Pakistani Prime Minister, Liaqat Ali Khan, only rubbed salt into their wounds when he told them to be content with their old job of driving donkeys.

The Sindhi rejection of Pakistan is total, and ideological. Mr. G.M. Syed, who once presided over the Sindh Muslim League, and introduced Pakistan Resolution in Sindh Assembly, became the uncrowned king of Sindh. His slogan: "Pakistan must die, if Sindh is to live." And he formulated a whole philosophy of a separate and sovereign Sindh. According to Mr. Syed refugees have misappropriated Hindu properties, mostly on the basis of faked claims. He accused the Punjabis of usurping, in the name of ex-servicemen, Sindhi lands irrigated by the two new barrages. And he points out that Sindhis have only three per cent representation in the central services.

Today Syed Saheb is dead but Sindh is following in his footsteps. They challenge the very Islamic basis of Pakistan. Partition, they argued, goes counter to the geography, history and culture of Sindh. While they are all for the Islamic principles of unity of God and equality of man they are not prepared to accept 'Arab-chhaap Islam' as advocated by the fundamentalists. They ridicule the Haj pilgrimage and say that the water of the Indus is much better than that of the sacred Arab well of *Zam Zam*. They even go so far as to say that if Sindhis have to choose between Islam and Sindhiat (Sindhi identity) they would prefer their country to their church. According to them, "Sindh rejects the Arabian edition of Islam; it rejects the Punjabi version of Pakistan, and it rejects made-in-India Urdu. Iqbal and Jinnah have been worse disasters for Muslims than Chenghez and Halaku. Sindh rejects them both". The new hero of Sindhi Muslims is Raja Dahir Sen, the last Hindu ruler of the province; Mohammed bin Qasim is regarded as the villain. Even the RSS in pre-Partition Sindh did not glorify Dahir Sen to this extent.

Sindhis further say: "A Sufi Sindh and an Islamic Pakistan cannot co-exist—even as you cannot put two swords in one

scabbard. If Pakistan continues, Sindh will die. If, therefore, Sindh is to live, Pakistan must die." The typical Sindhi argument is: "We have been Sindhi for 5,000 years, Muslim for 500 years, Pakistani for 50 years." It is thus evident that Sindhi rejection of Pakistan is basic and total.

Two questions arise: how strong is Sindhi separatist feeling? And can it prevail against the state of Pakistan? It seems to me that separatism is the majority feeling. Some elderly Sindhi Muslims go so far as to greet each other with "Ram-Ram". A few Sindhi Muslim girls are even seen sporting a *bindi*. The most popular feminine name is Marui, a patriotic heroine of Sindhi folklore; a runner-up name is 'Sindhu'.

It is obvious that Sindhis cannot face the army in pitched battles, but they can play havoc by sabotage and guerilla action. The Hurs, for example, made it so tough for the British in the early Forties that the latter had to declare martial law in half of Sindh for more than two years. In any case, the army cannot extinguish the Sindhi identity by force. In the long run, the Sindhi nationalist will prevail over the Punjabi gun.

The question for India is whether New Delhi has any role to play in all this. The answer is both, no and yes. India has no role to play in spreading dissatisfaction in Pakistan. But a democratic India cannot allow the democratic aspirations of Sindhis—and Baluchis and Pathans and even the Punjabis—to be crushed by the dictatorial agents of a remote foreign power. (Interestingly enough the USA is even more unpopular in Pakistan than it is in India.) If, as and when, therefore, these communities show unmistakable signs of birthpangs, India cannot but act as the good midwife. That is at once our right and our duty as a good neighbour. It will then be for these new states to decide, in freedom, whether they would like to have any particular relationship with each other, or with India, and, if so, what.

□

India, Pakistan and the Bomb

Pakistan is only a fault-line
between India and West Asia.

When India staged a series of nuclear tests on May 11, 1998—and again on May 13—a wave of joy and pride swept the country. When on May 28 Pakistan staged its series of nuclear tests, we felt a bit pushed, a bit threatened.

There was good enough reason for uneasiness on our side. India and Pakistan have had an adversarial relationship ever since the birth of Pakistan. We have even had four wars. In this situation it was natural for Pakistan to fear the Indian Bomb—and for India to fear the Pakistani Bomb. However, in the midst of this mutual antipathy, we overlooked the deeper significance of the two tests. Here was a double challenge to the five nuclear powers who have been lording it over the world since the end of World War II.

Obviously in the context of our prolonged differences, we could not congratulate each other on our respective tests. But history will no doubt view the India-Pakistan tests of May 1998 as historic. While in the short term they constitute, for India and Pakistan, a deterrent to each other, in the long term they constitute a double assertion of the importance of the Hindustan Peninsula. It is, therefore, quite possible that, now that both India and Pakistan have graduated as nuclear weapons states, we will increasingly think and act as mature states and take a mountain-top view of things.

Nor do we have to think of only nuclear bombs when

considering nuclear policy. The fact of the matter is that atoms and rockets and computers and satellites are all frontiers of science and technology. They are also the Big Business of the 21st century. The USA is opposed to a nuclear India not because it is afraid of an Indo-Pak nuclear war. Their chief worry is that a scientifically advanced India could be a great competitor in world trade in high-tech items. India could sell computers and satellites at a quarter of the American price.

Some friends think that the Indo-Pak nuclear confrontation will trigger an arms race which will cost billions of dollars. Nothing of the kind is going to happen. For one thing, nuclear arms are much cheaper than conventional arms like guns, tanks and planes. (The Pokhran II tests cost us less than Rs 1 crore.) For another, once you are nuclear, you cease to bother over much about conventional armour. Thirdly, over the last fifty years, India and Pakistan have come to acquire an arms balance of say 2:1. That being so, Pakistan cannot get the better of India; and India will not find Pakistan a pushover. This makes for a stable balance.

Nothing that Pakistan can do can cancel out this fact of Indian power. Should Pakistan try to match India—gun for gun, tank for tank, plane for plane and Bomb for Bomb—it will find the strain beyond its limits of toleration. Even as USSR broke up in its compulsive competition with the USA, Pakistan will break up if it launches itself on a course of competition with India. It is significant that the new Indian budget increases the defence budget by only 13 per cent—just to cover the annual inflation rate and the Pay Commission recommendations. And the next Pakistan budget is not likely to be very different in this respect.

Also it is good to remember that India and Pakistan have never fought a long war. Iran and Iraq fought for eight years; India and Pakistan have never fought for even one full month! It is significant that we have never destroyed each other's bridges or barrages. It would seem that, with all our antipathies, we recognise, in the inmost recesses of our mind that, after all we are One People. The Pakistanis are much closer to Indians than they are to Arabs, Iranians or Turks. In the global context—in the language of

Prof. Huntington of 'Clash of Civilizations' fame—Pakistan is only a 'fault-line' between 'Hindu' India and 'Muslim' West Asia.

Some friends think that China is the bigger enemy. Actually words like "enemy"—bigger or smaller—need to be eschewed in a serious discussion. It would be truer to say that we have problems with China and Pakistan—and these problems need to be amicably resolved. Having said that, I must make it clear that we have a much stronger love-hate relationship with Pakistan than with China. When tensions are high, we heartily hate Pakistan; but otherwise, and at the personal level, we are the best of friends. When, however, it comes to China, neither our friendship nor our hostility go very deep. The relationship is remote. Don't forget the Himalaya!

When China attacked India in 1962, Pakistan first sided with India. It was only when Pakistan and China saw that they could use each other as a lever against India in their respective problems with India, that they began to join hands. And the USA was only too happy to fish in these troubled waters. It was already using Muslim Pakistan—along with a 'Jewish' Israel—to police Muslim West Asia. Two Pakistani divisions protected the Saudi King from his own people. And it was Pakistan's Zia who slaughtered Palestinians in Jordan at US instance, breaking the heart of Nasser, and earning for himself the future Presidency of Pakistan.

It will be remembered that Kissinger secretly flew to Beijing from Pakistan. The USA used Pakistan to intervene in Afghanistan, and it is now using the same route to knock at the doors of oil-rich Central Asia. The USA has not only been arming Pakistan, it has been letting China arm Pakistan. But its great game does not end there. While Pakistan wants Kashmir for itself, USA wants Kashmir to be *Azad* (independent) so that it can use the strategic valley as a base to keep an eye on India, China, Iran, Russia, Pakistan, Central Asia in the 21st century. And now the Sept. 11, 2001 attacks on World Trade Center in New York and Pentagon in Washington, have radically transformed the world scene.

It will thus be seen that it is the USA which is playing politics in Asia—and indeed all over the world—and exploiting regional

problems to promote its own global interests. While China's occupation of Tibet was wrong, the USA compounded the problem by overflying Indian territory and dropping arms and anti-Chinese literature in Tibet, and flying out Khampas for military training in the USA. It is not known whether the Nehru Government was unable or unwilling to stop these American activities, which were irritating China. It is also learnt that the CIA misled India's Intelligence Bureau about Chinese military presence and preparedness in Tibet. It was under this wrong impression that Nehru ordered the Indian troops to "throw out" the Chinese from Thagla Ridge.

A question here arises why the USA tends to side with China and not with India. For one thing USA and China are each other's nextshore neighbours—across the Pacific Ocean. For another, the USA has had a much longer relationship with China than with India. Very few Indians had visited USA and very few Americans had visited India before 1947. American missionaries have been at work in China for more than a hundred years. Chinese labour had helped build the American railway system. It is significant that while Pearl Buck wrote *Good Earth* in appreciation of China, another American author, Katherine Mayo, wrote *Mother India*, denouncing India.

The USA finds it much easier to work with dictatorial regimes than with democratic regimes. In China, the USA has to deal only with the Chinese Government. Once Beijing lets in Coke, no Chinese will dare campaign against it. In India, the USA has not only to negotiate with New Delhi, it has also to listen to Opposition music and nationalist aspirations. And these can often checkmate US business interests. And so, notwithstanding American claims to favour democracy, it actually prefers dictators. Dictators are good for (US) business!

This does not mean that Indo-American relations will never mend. The USA feels at once more impressed with, and more threatened by China. On the other hand, in Indo-American relations, the English language provides a big link. So does the Indian legal system, based on Anglo-Saxon law. Indian dancing

and *Yoga* and *Gurus* charm the Americans no end. As India picks up economically and militarily, it is going to command greater respect in the West.

There is, therefore, nothing to worry. We don't have to bother about the G-5 or anybody else wanting us to settle for mediation on Kashmir. The UK has had the Irish problem for centuries. Did they ever invite or accept any mediation? Recently when they worked out a settlement, President Clinton just wanted to go and bless it—for the edification of Irish Americans. But he was told to stay at home! India also should not even bother to respond to G-5. Let it, on the other hand, have the will and the vision to contact threshold countries and other middle powers along with Pakistan, and press for a new and juster world order.

□

The Burden of History

The Pakistan Press used to carry all kind of lies about India. Prime Minister Mohammed Ali told me that that was necessary for five years to build up the nation. When I told him India could retaliate, he said: "No I am not at all afraid. Your religion is not capable of fanaticism."

—B.K. Nehru
'Nice Guys Finish Second'

Don't forget, Minister, that every Indian carries the burden of a thousand years of history.

—Inder Kumar Gujral to Yaqub,
Foreign Minister of Pakistan

Tell me what is the difference between you and the Indians. You look alike to me. Are you not only temporarily separated from the Indians?

—Mao Tse-tung to Pakistan
Foreign Minister Arshad Hussain 1971

Pakistan says it feels incomplete without Kashmir. India feels incomplete without Pakistan.

—A.B. Vajpayee

Some Lessons of Agra

Apart from P.O.K., there is Pak-Occupied Sindh and Pak-Occupied Baluchistan.

The Agra Summit has left a lingering bad taste in the mouth. Many, many questions arise.

The Government of India had originally rightly taken the position that there will be no India-Pakistan talks until and unless the cross-border terrorism ended. Why did we decide to invite General Musharraf when that terrorism was still very much on?

General Musharraf said we had invited him under American pressure. New Delhi denies it. And now the American Press has found fault with India for rejecting "three drafts". What are these drafts? Who had drafted them? Or are we back to that bad old American 'tilt to Pakistan' days?

China and Russia have also been having serious problems for almost half a century. Recently they met for just four hours and signed a historic Treaty of Friendship. Why did we invite Musharraf—and even fix the dates of the Summit—when there was no Declaration ready for signing—and no agreement even on agenda?

It is public knowledge that India wholly disapproved of Pakistan's idea of inviting the Hurriyat rebels to its Tea Party. (They did not invite anybody else from J&K State!). Could not New Delhi have made it clear to Pakistan that if the Hurriyat invitation was on, then the Agra invitation was off? And in any case why did we talk to Hurriyat chaps the following day?

The understanding was that if there was no joint statement, there would be no Press Conference. What was the propriety of the Pakistan leader inviting some Indian editors—leaving out even Doordarshan, Zee TV and UNI—and showing on television an "informal breakfast"? Was it not possible for the good host to make the General act the good guest?

Pakistan made much of Sushma Swaraj's brief press briefing. But if they indeed found it wanton, why did they take ten hours to react? Is it a fact that it was only the feed-back from Islamabad, duly peppered by Pakistan Foreign Minister Abdul Sattar, that caused the General to take belated umbrage? His agressive posture in his breakfast meeting with Indian editors has sent his popularity graph soaring in Pakistan. It would seem that the General had not come here to improve relations with India but to improve his standing back home. It is significant that both the major parties in Pakistan—Pakistan People's Party and Pakistan Muslim League—are opposed to his military dictatorship. We have not exactly served the democratic interests of the people of Pakistan by hurriedly greeting the self-appointed President of Pakistan and lionising him.

Rather late in the day, Government has said Agra is dead and we must in future start from Shimla and Lahore. The question is: Why did we forget Shimla and Lahore on the eve of Agra? Why did we not make it publicly clear to the Government and people of Pakistan that in Agra we will have to build on Shimla and Lahore?

One wishes Government did not maintain a studied silence on the many misleading statements made by General Musharraf in Delhi. He said that India had violated the Shimla Agreement by occuping Siachin Glacier. He also said that we had very much hurt Pakistan by the 1971 war. He went on to say that the terrorism in Kashmir was not being exported by Pakistan; that it was a war of liberation like the one being fought by Palestinians. He also glibly said that democracy had never existed in Pakistan and that the fate of Kashmir must be decided by the people of Kashmir.

At the Shimla Conference, Siachin area had been left undemarcated as uninhabitable. It was only because Pakistan entertained a mountaineering expedition application for Siachin

that India went and occupied it—to forestall any Pakistani claim on the basis of precedent.

The 1971 war came because Pakistan was not willing to accept its 1971 election results and allow Mujibur Rehman to assume office. The Shia Lobby and USA wanted a Pakistan-Iran (and, if possible)-Turkey Confederation and, to this end, they made war on the people of Bangladesh, sent over ten million refugees to India, and drove East Bengal to secession. (In their anxiety to counter-balance India, they did not pause to ponder that Iran was Shia and Pakistan and Turkey Sunni; that they belonged to three different races; that they had different interests; and that, in addition, Iran and Turkey did not share Pakistan's hatred of India.) India had no choice but to go and restore law and order on its eastern border.

Pakistan invokes the UN resolutions *ad nauseum*. What do these resolutions say? They say that Pakistan side shall withdraw all its troops from PoK; that PoK shall be handed over to the lawfully constituted Government of J& K State; that at that stage India will withdraw bulk of its forces; after that the two countries will enter into consultations to determine fair and equitable conditions to know the will of the people. Has Pakistan at any stage fulfilled any of these conditions?

Today Pakistan is not only exporting terrorism to Kashmir, it is recruiting, importing, training, arming and financing terrorists to carry mayhem into Kashmir. It would seem Pakistan is determined to fight India to the last Kashmiri.

That the future of Kashmir should be decided by Kashmiris sounds axiomatic but here many complex questions arise. The Independence of India Act established the States of India and Pakistan. The Princely States were asked to choose between India and Pakistan. There was no third option of 'Independence'.

While the Congress wanted States People to make the choice, the Muslim League came out for the Princes to make the decision. (They had hoped to secure the accession of 'Muslim' States like Hyderabad, Junagarh etc.) In the case of Jammu, Kashmir and Ladakh State, not only the Prince signed for India, the people opted for India by acclaim. It was the people of Kashmir who gave the

call *Hamlawar Ho Khabardar Hum Kashmiri Hain Tayar* (Beware you raiders: We Kashmiris are ready to face you). And it was they who helped the Army stop and push back the raiders from Pakistan. Subsequently, thanks to Pakistani propaganda, heavy arming and even heavier financing, and foreign interest, the Kashmiris today are in three minds—Indian, Pakistani and Independent. The *Azadi-wallahs'* slogan is: *Pakistan Ka Yaar, Kashmir ka Gaddar* i.e. friends of Pakistan are enemies of Kashmir. And an independent Kashmir will become a foreign base to keep an eye on India, Pakistan, Iran, China, Russia and Central Asia!

Issues settled in terms of the Indian Independence Act cannot be reopened at will and at random. And if one issue is opened, many more will open up. In 1947, NWFP was not given the choice of Independence. Many Pathans boycotted the Plebiscite because they had no choice; their province, not being contiguous to India, could not possibly accede to India.

The fate of Sindh was sealed by a divided anti-League vote. The Province was 70% Muslim and 30% Hindu. In the early 1946 General elections 30% Hindus voted for Congress; 30% Muslims voted for the parties of Nationalist Muslim Leaders G.M. Syed and Maula Bux; and only 40% Muslims voted for Muslim League. In any Plebiscite, Sindh would have opted for India. Baluchistan's future was decided by just the Municipal Committee of Quetta! Today there are independence movements in the two States which are being described, like the PoK (Pakistan-occupied Kashmir) as PoS (Pakistan-occupied Sindh) and PoB (Pakistan-occupied Baluchistan). What does the General have to say to that?

The General said Pakistan never had any democracy. This is not true. Pakistan's Constituent Assembly was as democratically elected as India's. It was the Military, backed by its foreign god-fathers, who dissolved that Constituent Assembly and started the political puppet show we see in Pakistan. His military predecessor Zia-ul-Haq said Allah had told him in a dream that "elections are un-Islamic". Do elections become un-Islamic in Pakistan and PoK, but Islamic in Kashmir?

Musharraf has done a secret commando course with USA's Green Berets at Fort Bragg. The commando in him, therefore, is

always to the fore. "The arts of dissimulation, subterfuge, deception and surprise are the qualities ingrained in a commando during training" notes B. Raman, a former Secretary in the Cabinet Secretariat. No wonder the Agra meet of gentleman-statesman Vajpayee and commando-President Musharraf went the way it did.

General Musharraf is on record that even the solution of the Kashmir issue will not solve India-Pakistan problems. He says India is big and hegemonist. Shall India cut itself down to Pakistan's size, for the General's comfort?

The reality is that Kashmir is a by-product of Partition; and Partition itself was the result of a campaign of hatred against Hindus, Hinduism and India. Until and unless Pakistan is cured of this pathological hatred, no lasting peace is possible. But the trouble is that this hatred is being fostered all the time through Pakistani media and history books. For example, school children in Pakistan are taught that Hindus had no culture and no civilization before Islam; that in the 1965 war, India suffered ten times more casualties than Pakistan; that before 1947, "India was part of our country" that is Pakistan; and that next only to Arabic, Urdu is the most popular language in the world, ahead even of English. Mr. K.K. Aziz has rightly titled his critique of the text books used in Pakistan as *The Murder of History* (Vanguard, Karachi). How exactly do you deal with a country brought up on such piffle?

The Shimla Agreement with Bhutto was killed by Bhutto himself. The Bus Diplomacy with Nawaz Sharrif was aborted by Musharraf. It would seem that serious negotiations are not possible with the rudderless Pakistan unless that State is jointly represented by its Prime Minister, Leader of Opposition and Army Chief.

In Shimla we released 93,000 Pakistani POWs on Bhutto's word *Aap mujh par bharosa keejiye* ('please trust my word'- that we will never again raise Kashmir issue). Later his friend Humayun Gauhar told Mrs. Gandhi's Principal Private Secretary Shri P.N. Dhar: "Face it, Mr. Dhar, Mr. Bhutto fooled your Prime Minister." Let it not be said of any future India-Pakistan dealings that Pakistan fooled the Government of India.

□

VI. HINDU-MUSLIM EQUATION

Hindus & Muslims—Images & Identities

Mir-e-Arab Ko aayee, Thandhi hawa jahan se
Mera Watan wahi hai, Mera Watan wahi hai.

—*Iqbal on Prophet's view of India*

When we set out to improve Hindu-Muslim relations, we don't have to only dismantle Hindu-Muslim hostile images; we have to take note of, and tackle, the fact of historical hostility. The Hindu-Muslim hostility is not so much religious as it is civilizational. For as Al Biruni noted almost a thousand years ago: "The Hindus differ from us in every respect." However in this mortal titanic conflict, Hinduism and Islam both survived, though much influenced and changed by each other.

The large size, huge population and decentralised structure of India made it impossible for invaders to over-turn India completely—as they had over-turned ancient Egypt and Iran. India was also served well in this struggle by the caste system which acted as a social fortification; by the joint family which ensured social welfare; and by the Panchayat system which rendered every village a proud little republic. And on top of this there was the Hindu's consciousness of the worth of his thought, his ways and his values. That is how India survived as basically a Hindu country, bloodied but unbowed.

In this prolonged inter-face, Islam profoundly influenced Hindu India in every respect, including religious. A struggling

Hindu India even gave itself warrior-gods like Rama and Krishna—in place of traditional 'natural' gods like Surya, Agni, Vayu and Varuna. But the pervasive Hindu atmosphere of accommodation also transformed the invader. The fact that the local converts had a strong Hindu cultural background further helped Hindu-Muslim adjustment. Before long Kabir was preaching Hindu-Muslim unity. And Amir Khusro switched from Persian, Arabic and Turkic to Hindavi—as Hindi was then called—to make himself intelligible at least to his *Nani* (maternal grand-mother) who was an Indian convert to Islam. Shivaji and Guru Govind Singh revolted against Aurangzeb, not because he was a Muslim but because he was a tyrant. Both of them said that, had Aurangzeb's elder brother, Dara Shikoh, become king, there would have been no problem; all would have been well.

This progressive integration of Hindu and Islamic streams manifested itself in 1857 when Hindus and Muslims fought shoulder to shoulder against the British. Our modern Hindu-Muslim problems are rooted in subsequent British policy.

1857 convinced the British that they could not rule India for very long. They, therefore, decided to divide the Indian people, in a cynical bid to stretch their rule as long as possible. The Hindu-Muslim divide, the Hindu-Sikh differentiation, the North-South dichotomy, the 'upper' caste-'lower' caste syndrome, the theory that India had always been ruled by invaders etc., were all worked out by British rulers. Curzon candidly described it all as "the furniture of empire". Before 1857, the British had three Armies in India—Bengal Army, Bombay Army, Madras Army—organised on territorial lines. Since the Army had revolted, it was reorganised on caste and community lines. The seeds of our current divisions and dissensions had been duly planted.

1905 proved as crucial as 1857. In that year educated India voiced its demand for *Swadeshi* and *Swaraj*. The British promptly interpreted the demand for Independence as demand for "Hindu Raj", to scare the Muslims. After 1857 they had divided the Army on communal lines. After 1905 they divided the whole country on communal lines—and introduced separate electorates, reservations

and weightages. The result was Partition and the murderous unpleasantness that went with it.

How do we reverse this recent course of history: that is the question. There are no easy ways out of this imbroglio. It has to be a long and slow but sure process of re-education and re-orientation. We cannot effect change of Hindu and Muslim hearts by white-washing unpleasant facts. We must be adult enough to face facts. The British in their eagerness to divide Hindus and Muslims projected only negative facts. We need to take note of all significant facts, both negative and positive, and prepare the coming generations to work out a peaceful and purposeful coexistence. While facts—even negative facts—are sacred, and must not be suppressed, we must clear old misconceptions and work for a maturer understanding of historic processes.

Although the Hindu believes in *Sarva Dharma Sama Bhava* (equal respect for all religions), he does not mentally accept the equal validity of Islam. There are two reasons for this: Islam spread in India with the sword; and the Hindu does not concede any role to violence in matters religious. Secondly, the axiom *Sarva Dharma Sama Bhava* was enunciated in relation to the fraternity of Indian creeds—from Buddhism and Jainism to Veerashaivism and Sikhism—which share the same idiom and the same set of values. This Sanatan formulation was never intended to cover a very different kind of credal semitic religion like Islam.

However, the fact of Muslim power and Hindu tolerance gave the two societies the time and the opportunity to adjust to each other and settle down. Additionally, the Hindu-Muslim relationship in India has a redeeming feature. The Prophet of Islam knew about India and liked India. He had said he got cool breezes from India. Iqbal translated this sentiment in the memorable couplet:

Mir-e-Arab ko ayee, Thandhi hawa jahan se,
Mera Watan wahi hai, Mera Watan wahi hai.

He once greeted his wife Hinda—also known as 'Um-Salma'—with the words: "May Allah bless the country after which you are named."

Many Muslims in India think that 'Green' is the flag of Islam.

It is not. It was the flag of Turks who invaded India. The Prophet had no particular flag. He carried different flags in his numerous campaigns. And it so happens that he never carried a green flag but he did once carry a saffron flag.

In the *Hadis*, Prophet Mohammed is quoted as saying: "Cow's flesh is poison; cow's milk is medicine."

Unfortunately none of these facts are known at large or mentioned in our history books. Knowledge of these facts could build a golden bridge of understanding between Hindus and Muslims from childhood onwards.

Hindus believe that Muslims forcibly converted Hindus and that they did not take part in the freedom movement. Both these impressions are only half-true. Many Hindus were no doubt forcibly converted. But many converted to Islam to bask in the sunshine of state patronage. And many others—particularly Buddhists in East Bengal—converted to Islam as a result of the sheer morbidity of the society there.

Also, according to Max Weber, the great sociologist, during Muslim rule, the number of tribals who entered the Sanatan Hindu fold was greater than the number of Hindus who went out and embraced Islam. This situation is reminiscent of West Asia where, even five hundred years after the birth of Islam, some 40% people had remained non-Muslim; it was only the pressure of Christian Crusades that persuaded the non-Muslims to embrace Islam as the religion of national resistance to foreign invasion! Saladin, who resisted the crusades most, was not even an Arab; he was a Kurd!

As for the Freedom Movement, Muslims opposed British Rule as much as the Hindus. And both in 1857 and 1921, Muslims were more prominent in the Freedom Movement than Hindus. Apart from Maulana Azad and Rafi Ahmed Kidwai, the contribution of Justice Badruddin Tyabji, G.M. Bhurgri, Mazhar-ul-Haque, Hakim Ajmal Khan, Dr. Ansari, Tassaduq Sherwani, Ali brothers, Umar Sobhani, Allah Bux Soomro, Ashfaque-ullah, Khan brothers, Maulana Hasrat Mohani, Maulana Obaidullah Sindhi and even of Mr. Jinnah until 1937, to the Freedom Movement, is second to none.

Our Muslim brethren also suffer from many misconceptions. Today they think that Dussehra and Diwali, Vasant and Holi are Hindu festivals. The Mughals didn't think so; they viewed them as people's festivals and celebrated them with *eclat* as National Festivals.

Some Muslims ridicule caste system. Good or bad, casteism is about as prevalent among Muslims as among Hindus. No Ashraf ('Upper'-caste Muslim) like Syed, Khan, Shaikh would think of marrying an Arzal ('lower'-caste Muslim).

Many Indian Muslims think they ruled India for centuries. It was the various Turkish tribes and dynasties—and not Indian Muslims—that ruled India. Indian Muslims had about as much role under Turkish rule as Indian Christians had under British rule.

Today many Muslims make an issue of 'Muslim Law'. However, until 1937, a majority of Indian Muslims lived by Customary Law. Many Muslims also argue about Urdu versus Hindi. Here again fact is that Urdu is 75% Hindi and even many letters of the Arabic Script are based on the Brahmi Script. Dr. Mumtaz Hussain Pathan, Pakistani scholar agreed with Pandit Satwalekar on this issue and said: "Thc Arabic Script which is supposed to have been borrowed from the Nabataeans, was greatly influenced by the Hindu Nagari Script."

A reorientation of the Hindu and Muslim minds on the above objective and balanced lines could, before long, provide an abiding basis for a final and amicable solution of the Hindu-Muslim problem.

I'm afraid much of the disputation is semantic; it is a dispute about the connotation of terms like 'Hindu'. Perhaps a reformulation of these terms could help. For example while religiously, Hindus would be Hindu, and Muslims, Muslim, all Indians could be described as 'Hindustani'. (Indian pilgrims to Mecca have always been known as 'Hindi' after our country, 'Hind'.) The 'Hindi' language could be re-christened as Bharati, or 'Hindavi', as it was known five hundred years ago. And the country could be called 'Hindustan' as before, and not evasively as 'Bharat'.

We need to be guided in this matter by Mahatma Gandhi and Sri Aurobindo. Gandhiji had said: "There is in Hinduism room enough for Jesus, as there is for Mohammed, Zoroaster and Moses." And Sri Aurobindo's masterly advice was: "Hindu-Mohammedan unity cannot be effected by political adjustment or Congress flatteries. It must be sought deeper down, in the heart and in the mind, for where the causes of disunion are, there the remedies must be sought...We should remember that love compels love and that strength conciliates strength. We must strive to remove the causes of misunderstanding by a better mutual knowledge and sympathy; we must extend the unfaltering love of the patriot to our *Mussalman* brother, remembering that to him too our Mother has given a permanent place in her bosom; but we must cease to approach him falsely or flatter him out of a selfish weakness and cowardice...We shall make it a main part of our work to place Mohammed and Islam in a new light before our readers, to spread juster views of Mohammedan history and civilization, to appreciate the *Mussalman's* place in our national development and the means of harmonising his communal life with our life. What is wanted is some new religious movement among the Mohammedans which would remodel their religion and change the stamp of their temperament" (Karmayogin Vol. 2, p. 24).

The tragedy of the situation is that without going to the root of the problem, politicians have been indulging in cheap gimmicks. What this country needs more than anything else is a true and balanced history of India. Once that gets going, it will become increasingly clear to all that Hindus, Muslims and Christians of India, Pakistan and Bangladesh are basically One People. And once this consciousness grows the way will be clear for India to emerge as the top country in the world.

□

Some Muslim Grievances

Justice for All; Appeasement of None.

—*The BJP Creed*

Our secularist friends are beginning to concede that Hindus in India do have some genuine grievances concerning Partition, declaration of Pakistan and Bangladesh as Islamic States when India stays 'secular', Muslim opposition to a Uniform Civil Law, etc. But they insist that Muslim grievances have "more substance". In this connection it is alleged that "they are poor, much more so than the average Hindu. Very few of them have any land. They make up only 1.5 per cent of the bureaucracy when they are 12 per cent of the population. They are equally under-represented in the Legislatures, Armed Forces and the private corporate sector."

Now we are not exactly living in an egalitarian society. That kind of equality is found only in tribal societies. Louis Dumont writes in his book *Homo Hierarchicus* that man is by nature a believer in hierarchy or 'caste'. There is no equality even in a communist society. Ever since the institution of property developed—first in herds of cattle and, later, in land—there has been inequality among individuals and societies. Indeed, hierarchy and civilization have everywhere gone together. The important thing, therefore, to consider is not whether the average Muslim is worse off than the average Hindu (the average Bihari and Oriya is poorer than the average Gujarati and Punjabi), but whether the Hindu is responsible for the relative poverty of the Muslim.

I am afraid that, other things being equal, the Muslim is likely to be poorer because he tends to spend more where the Hindu is inclined to save—and invest—more. It is a matter of habit or tradition. Also the Muslim family tends to be large. There is, therefore, less to go round. As for land ownership, we used to have a higher percentage of Muslim *Zamindars*. With *Zamindari* and *Jagirdari* abolition, all landlords, Hindu and Muslim, lost their lands above a certain ceiling, to their tenants, Hindu and Muslim. So what is the complaint about? Is anybody against *Zamindari* abolition?

As for jobs, the situation is more complex. In the Government of India there is no reservation, except for SC and ST. Everybody else has to compete for jobs. (As a result some regions and sections have a lesser presence in the Services than some others.) At the time of Partition almost all Muslim Government employees opted for Pakistan. The Muslim educated elite by and large migrated to Pakistan. No wonder not many Muslims remaining in India are able to compete successfully for jobs.

The basic reason for this is lack of education. Although Muslims are some 12% of the population, Muslim children constitute only about 2% of the Indian school population. The basic question, therefore, is; why don't they attend school?

There could be many reasons. Many Hindu communities—Brahmins, Khatris, Kayasths, Banias—have had a long tradition of education. In the Muslim society, except for the religious instruction of the *Maulanas*, such a tradition is weak. When the British came, Hindus took avidly to English education; Muslims did not. It was thought that English education would weaken their faith.

In Independent India also they are wary of education. A Muslim friend tells me they fear that Hindu-oriented school texts would de-Islamise Muslim students. That Indian school books have a 'Hindu' orientation would be news to Vishwa Hindu Parishad. But assuming this to be the case, a little 'Hinduisation' will only make co-existence with Hindus easier for Muslims. As the old saying goes, 'Do in Rome as the Romans do.' In the alternative, why don't they start their own schools, with Government aid, under Article 30 of the Constitution?

I think the real reasons for educational backwardness among Muslims are different. Most of them are artisans. Their children can start earning and learning at an early age. They do not therefore find it worth their while to send their children to school and college, spend thousands on their education and upbringing, and then look for jobs which are not easy for anybody to come by.

As for unemployment, there is no reason to believe that it is more rampant among Muslims. Only the Employment Exchange can throw some light on the matter. But in any case, unemployment, whether among Hindus or Muslims, is the result of a mismanaged economy. If, however, Muslims are in fact being discriminated against in the matter of jobs, that is wholly wrong. Somebody should study the matter and come out with facts. Nobody wants any injustice to be done to any section of the population. Our credo must be "Justice for All; Appeasement of None."

When it comes to business, apart from Bohras, Khojas and Memons of Gujarat, the generality of Muslims have never been prominent in trading activities. Even during Muslim rule, from Khiljis to Mughals, business was mostly in Hindu hands.

Whether it was Allauddin Khilji or Timurlang, Akbar or Aurangzeb, their cashiers and treasurers were invariably Hindus. Historian Badauni noted in his *Tarikh-e-Firuzshahi*, that Hindu traders were "rolling in wealth". Even Aurangzeb used to borrow money from Hindu bankers.

When the British came, they also found it easier to do business with Hindus than with Muslims. Wrote Clive: "These fat expensive Moormen (Muslims) spend Government's revenue in luxury and assuagements. Indeed, in my opinion, none but *Gentoos* (a corruption of the Portuguese word 'Gentio' i.e. gentile or heathen for Hindu) ought to be renters of counters who always spend less than their income and can, when called upon, make good any deficiency in the revenues."

This, in brief, is the history of Muslim weakness in business. It is for them to go deep into the matter and do the needful to mend matters. Meanwhile it is happy to note that today the richest Indian is a Muslim gentleman, Premji Azim.

As regards the Police and the Army, Muslims used to be over-represented in these branches before Independence. It is possible that they are under-represented today. Part of the reason could be that modern soldiering requires more brain, that is education, than brawn. Another part-reason could also be the wariness of the military establishment to pit Muslim soldiers against Pakistani troops. In any case, if Muslims have not been having their due share in the Police and the Military, the responsibility rests with the Government which has been run from the Day of Independence by 'Secularists', and not with the 'communalists' who have been kept out of even civilian jobs through Home Ministry circular against 'RSS'. It is a secular complaint against 'secularists'; the 'communalists' don't come into this picture.

Yet another grievance often heard in Muslim circles is that they don't have due representation. This is not quite true. It is true enough that we don't have 12% Muslim legislators in the country. But there are probably 25% 'Hindu' legislators who are there on the strength of Muslim votes! Muslims vote as avidly as anybody else; many times they vote *en bloc*; as a result Muslim interests come to be specially represented by many more than 12% legislators.

As for joining the national mainstream, say the secularists, a young Muslim can do so only by foregoing enough of his cultural heritage to allay the suspicions of Hindu young man. Hindu and Muslim are both gradually foregoing their respective cultural heritage before the tide of Westernism. Why should the Muslim youngster mind doing in India as Hindu neighbours do it—'doing in Rome as the Romans do it'?

This is a very old debate in India. And the great Sufi Saint Gesudaraz told Muslim Indians centuries ago that many of the practices they were following were Turkish, and not Islamic. Let the Muslim Indian do his Islamic Roza, Namaz, Haj, Zakat etc., and, for the rest, be Indian, act Indian—and there will be no problem for him or for others.

□

Are Hindus Getting a Raw Deal?

If Jana Sangha is communal then
I am also communal.

—*Jaya Prakash Narain*

The secularists are surprised by what they describe as 'Hindu Fundamentalism' and 'Hindu Backlash'. They wonder what it is and why it is. India is well over 80% Hindu; and we have a democratic system of government. In the polity, the economy, the society, most people at the top are 'Hindu'. So, what more do Hindus want? And yet many Hindus are saying that Hindus are getting a raw deal; and hundreds of millions of Hindus agree. So what is the matter? What is happening?

India was partitioned on the basis of religion. Pakistan has become an Islamic State—and so has Bangladesh. Some Hindus ask: Why can't India be Hindu? Why does it have to swear by 'Secularism' all the time? No secularist has a satisfactory answer to that.

Gandhiji had said in 1921 that cow protection is more important than even *Swaraj*. The Indian Constitution also provides for it. But to this day cattle continues to be slaughtered—through many loopholes in the law. (And now beef—and pork—is to be imported!) The Hindu notes it and does not like it.

Article 44 of the Constitution lays down as a Directive Principle of State Policy that India shall have a Uniform Civil Law. But even fifty years after the adoption of the Constitution, there is no trace of such a Law because Muslim Indians are not willing.

The Hindus ask: If Ayub Khan could ban polygamy and instant *talaq* by ordinance, why can't we? Why does India have to be more 'Islamic' than even Pakistan? Again there is no convincing response from the secular side.

Article 370 of the Constitution gives a special status to Jammu and Kashmir State. However, it also makes it clear that this special provision is purely 'temporary and transitional'. The Hindu asks: Was it not an act of communalism in the first place to give a special status to this state just because it had a slight Muslim majority? And why has this temporary provision become almost permanent? Once again the secularists have many excuses but no explanation.

Article 30 of the Constitution permits minorities—that is Muslims and Christians—to run educational institutions of their choice. That's okay. But the Constitution does *not* permit Hindus—or their various sects—to run their own educational institutions. As a result when the Ramakrishna Mission Schools were harassed by West Bengal's Communist Government, the R.K. Mission declared itself a non-Hindu minority, just to escape government control. Many Hindus were shocked. The Hindu asks: why can't the Hindus run their own schools—like Muslims and Christians—with Government grant, but without interference from the State? Once again the secularists have no answer. No Government has had the wit or wisdom to amend the Constitution to say that any religious community or sect shall be free to run educational institutions and impart religious instruction of its choice.

Nor is the Hindu feeling of a raw deal confined to matters of law and constitution. They experience it again and again in their daily life. A few years back there was a mass conversion to Islam in Meenakshipuram, Tamil Nadu. Few things have shocked Hindus more in recent years than Meenakshipuram. The question uppermost in the Hindu mind was: would any Muslims in Pakistan dare go Hindu, even if they wanted to? If not, why should the reverse process be permitted in India? Mr. Shahabuddin runs a magazine called *Muslim India* in Delhi. Would any Hindu dare publish *Hindu Pakistan* in Karachi? (There are over one million Hindus in Sindh alone.) was it not a case of Muslims winning the heads and Hindus

losing the tails?

The Freedom Movement was basically a movement for the emancipation and flowering of the Indian soul. The inspiration for it came from Swami Dayanand, Swami Vivekanand, Sri Aurobindo. This inspiration was given a political idiom by Tilak, Malaviya and Gandhi. But Independent India was hijacked by the Nehru Family.

India would have loved to have Subhas as Prime Minister. Britain wanted Nehru. And so Subhas was mysteriously removed from the scene. Between Nehru and Patel, even Congressmen wanted Patel. Not a single PCC in 1946 wanted Nehru as Congress President—the person who would become PM in 1947. And yet he elbowed his way to the top. And he remained there, with the support of Muslim and Marxist lobbies—and the joint blessings of UK, USA and USSR.

The Hindu felt cheated from Day One of Indian Independence. Where Gandhi and Patel, Bose and Prasad, CR and Azad had never run down RSS, Mr. Nehru and his brigade attacked it all the time. When he was asked to ban cow slaughter he said next he would be asked to ban horse-slaughter. During a mid-term poll in Andhra in the Fifties, Congress was pitted against Communists, but he attacked BJS—and not Communists. When the Telugu translators substituted CPI for BJP, the audience only smiled in amusement. For Nehru it was a fashion to ridicule Hindus and Hinduism.

In his last infamous meeting with IFS top brass in New Delhi in December 1963, he was asked how the Civil Services should handle Communists if they came to power at the Centre. And Nehru blew up: "Communists, Communists! Why are all of you so obsessed with Communists and Communism! The danger to India, mark you, is not Communism. It is Hindu right-wing communalism." Such was his pathological allergy to Hindus and Hinduism.

On one occasion he had even said that if he was ousted by Hindu communalists he would go abroad and fight them from there. A few questions arise: Is it a crime for a Hindu to think and act Hindu? If people in a free election choose to go right, left or middle, how is it the business of a PM to veto such a vote?

Nehru was fortunately followed by Lal Bahadur Shastri. Lal Bahadur soon became popular because people saw in him an authentic Indian. As the British Press remarked at the time, "underneath his white *khaddar* was the Hindu *geruva.*" But he too suddenly died—half as mysteriously as Bose.

And that opened the way for Nehru's daughter. Now she was not anti-Hindu on 'principle'; but she was pro-Muslim on political grounds. She depended upon the *Fatwas* of half a dozen *mullahs* to deliver the Muslim vote bank to her. And to impress the Muslims, she kept attacking RSS and BJP every other day.

Her son was a regular weather-cock. He had no conviction of any kind. When the Supreme Court expressed itself in the Shah Bano case in favour of a Uniform Civil Code, he welcomed that. But when Muslim extremists opposed that, he reversed the Shah Bano judgement itself by a new law. When he was visiting Syria, he 'thanked' that country for sending Mohammed Bin Qasim to invade Sindh in 712, 'with the message of Islamic brotherhood'. When Salman Rushdie wrote his *Satanic Verses*, India under Rajiv banned the book without reading it, before even Pakistan and Arabia.

Rajiv's successor, Mr. V.P. Singh, did not run down Hindus the Nehru way, but he pampered Muslims even more than Nehru. His closest friend was the incendiary Imam Bukhari. He decided to have Prophet Mohammed's birthday as holiday—which it is not even in Arabia or Pakistan—but not the birthdays of Rama and Krishna. He sanctioned Rs. 65 lacs for the repair of Jama Masjid Delhi, even though it is a rich, functioning mosque, owned by a Waqf, and not in the charge of the Archaeological Department. And on top of that he cheated the Hindus on Ayodhya.

Hindu asks: Why can't the Rama Janmabhoomi mandir, forcibly converted into a mosque, be re-constructed as a mandir? But the secularists are appalled; they think that will be communalism. The Hindu reaction is: If Ram Janmabhoomi is 'communal', so be it. As good old JP had said in 1975: "If Jana Sangha is communal then I am also communal."

Some of our Muslim brethren, aided and abetted by 'secularists' have been taking unreasonable postures from time to time. Even after the Government of India had banned *Satanic Verses* they took out an illegal anti-Salman Rushdie procession in Bombay, leading to over a dozen casualties. Years ago, when an Australian had tried to desecrate Al-Aqsa mosque in Jerusalem, Muslims in India took out processions shouting: *Jo Hum Se Takraega, Choor Choor Ho Jayega*. Hindus wondered if they were threatening the Jews who were not there, or the Hindus who were very much there?

In India, ceremonial functions begin with the lighting of *Mangal Deep*. There are Muslims who think the practice 'Hindu' and, therefore, 'not secular'. They are particularly unhappy when a Muslim Rashtrapati or Rajyapal lights a *Mangal Deep*.

In UK, ships are launched with the breaking of a bottle of champagne against the hull. In India we do it by breaking a coconut. Once again some Muslims find the coconut 'communal'. Shall we launch a ship with 'Khajoor', to be truly 'secular'?

A few years back a Hindi primary school text explained 'Ga' as the letter for 'Ganesh'. Some Muslims objected; and the 'Secularists' promptly had it changed to 'Ga' for *Gadha* (donkey).

The Hindu experiences these assinine secular pinpricks from time to time and is not amused.

Perhaps he could take even these pin-pricks in his stride. But along comes the 'Secularist' with his body blows. They attack Manu without reading Manu Samriti. They kill Sanskrit in school and college and then they say it is a 'dead language'. They stall Hindi on the excuse of 'Tamil objection'. They ridicule Rama and *Ramayana*. Mulayam Singh wanted Ram Janma Mandir built in Chitrakoot and not in Ayodhya. Laloo of Bihar asked on TV whether Rama was 'buried' at Janmabhoomi in Ayodhya. They long stalled Ramanand Sagar's tele-serial 'Krishna'. They object to *Bhajans* on Akashvani. The Civil Liberty-*Wallahs* and Democratic Rights-*Wallahs* shed copious tears when police shoot down terrorist killers; but they suddenly go deaf and dumb when Kashmiri Hindus are thrown out of Kashmir, or Ram-Bhaktas are mowed down in Ayodhya. These rootless 'Hindus' denounce Hindu organisations and ridicule Hindu *Dharma*. And yet these are the foreign-oriented people who rule India in the name of 'Secularism', 'Socialism' and 'Modernity'. Once again the Hindu is not amused by the posturings of these cultural self-abusers.

In this situation the Hindu feels cheated. He knows that India has been derailed and Indian Independence hijacked by foreign-oriented men and women. His stirrings over Ayodhya are something more than interest in brick and mortar. They are the stirrings of an ancient people trying to find their feet and recover their soul. When they are obstructed in this searching and striving by professional secularists they see it as a raw deal for our country, our people and our culture.

□

Mandirs-turned-Mosques

In the course of the first Russian occupation of Warsaw (1814-1915) the Russians had built an Eastern Orthodox Christian cathedral on this central spot in Warsaw that had been the capital of the once independent Roman Catholic Christian country, Poland. The Russians had done this to give the Poles a continuous ocular demonstration that the Russians were now their masters. After the re-establishment of Poland's independence in 1918, the Poles had pulled this cathedral down.

Aurangzeb's purpose in building those three mosques was the same intentionally offensive political purpose that moved the Russians to build their Orthodox cathedral in the city-centre at Catholic Warsaw. Those three mosques were intended to signify that an Islamic Government was reigning supreme, even over Hinduism's holiest of holy places. Perhaps the Poles were really kinder in destroying the Russians' self-discrediting monument in Warsaw than you have been in sparing Aurangzeb's mosques.

—Arnold Toynbee

Azad Memorial Lecture, New Delhi, 1960
'On World & India', page 60

A Day in Aligarh Muslim University

There is lot of history in myths
and lots of myth in history.

—Arnold Toynbee

Some time back the Aligarh Muslim University unit of the Students Islamic Organisation of India invited me to speak at a symposium on 'National Integration: Theory and Practice'. The SIO is the student front of the Jamaat-e-Islami. It is always a pleasure to meet bright, young religious-minded men. Many of them have strong views but these views are honestly held. After the symposium was over, many of them plied me with questions for the next two hours. Their questions gave me an insight into their thinking.

First of all they wanted it admitted that Islam had made a great contribution to civilization. It is true that as Muslim armies overran country after country, they carried the arts and sciences of every vanquished people far and wide. The resulting intermingling of cultures led to an explosion of knowledge, industry and commerce. For example, it was these armies that introduced sugar, silk, glass, steel, crop-rotation and gunpowder to Europe through the Crusaders. However, these armies were also great destroyers. Faced with their might, old cultures died. For example, the pre-Islamic language of Egypt is wholly lost to the world and Zoroastrianism was extinguished in Iran. It is difficult to draw up a balance sheet but this much is certain that while the destruction caused by Muslim armies is well-known, their intermingling of cultures, with its beneficent consequences, is not widely known or recognised.

Next these young men wanted to know whether Islam had not made a great contribution to India. Here again there are pluses and minuses. Obviously the five centuries of Muslim rule—from Mohammed Ghori to Aurangzeb—affected India widely and deeply. The big *bazaar*, *sadar*, even the *tandoors, biryanis* and *surahi* came from West Asia, not to mention the institutions of *Zamindari* and *Jagirdari*, for better or worse, which came with the Persians and Turks.

The Muslims also built monuments like the Taj Mahal, but they probably destroyed even more than they built. When Mahmud Ghazni was marching on Mathura, he was so bewitched by the beauty of golden domes and *shikharas* glistening in the morning sun that he ordered the whole army to stop and admire them, before ordering the city's destruction. Today there is not one single ancient temple standing anywhere in India except in the deep South. Wisdom demands that we take note of both the good and the bad. But the problem is that while many Hindus think that Muslim rulers did not do any good, many Muslims think that they did not do any bad. Few Muslims are prepared to condemn the excesses of Aurangzeb or Mahmud Ghazni. My young friends thought that conversions in India were mostly voluntary. I advised them to read Elliott and Dawson's *History of India as Told by its Historians*, all of them Muslim. Force was a big factor in conversions. The temptation of land and honours was also a major factor. But there were also voluntary conversions, mostly in East Bengal where a whole mass of Buddhists without the protection of caste, plumped for Islam after Buddhism declined as a force.

The young men in Aligarh wondered why Hindus looked upon the Aryan invasion as 'the advent of Aryans' but described the in-coming of Turks as 'Muslim invaders'. I had to tell them that the 'Aryan invasion' is only a theory propounded by British historians in the last century to justify British rule in India. These historians wanted to justify foreign rule by saying that the Turks who had ruled India were foreigners, and the Aryans who ruled India even earlier, were also aliens. There is no evidence—

historical, literary, archaeological or any other—about any such 'invasion'. There is no such race memory.

The Indus Valley civilization is supposed to be pre-Aryan and pre-Vedic. But you have the same Gods—Shiva, Kali etc—in Mohen-jo-daro, the same food habits, the same manner of dress, the same *havan-kunds.* The cephalic index of the shape of the skull shows that the inhabitants of Mohen-jo-daro had the same type of skull as modern Sindhis, and Lothal residents the same skull-shape as the modern Gujaratis. So much for the Aryan 'invasion'. There is no need to explain away and justify the crimes committed by the Turks and Mongols behind the smoke-screen of an Aryan 'invasion' that never was.

My young friends in AMU also thought that Islam had helped destroy caste and casteism in India. The position is exactly the opposite. Caste only became stronger in the face of the Islamic offensive. Caste was not just casteism and touch-me-not-ism. Caste was also a professional guild. Within a caste all men, rich and poor, were socially equal. Caste also meant social and economic security for caste-men. Caste, thus, was social fortification. In the violence and insecurity that followed the Turkish invasions, castes became more necessary, stronger, more important.

They also thought that Islam stands for equality. I told them that all religions stand for equality. The *Gita* even calls upon the wise to look with an equal eye on the Brahmin and the dog. But the practice is quite different. In the West the idea that all men are equal long meant only that all White Anglo-Saxon Protestant (WASPs) males are equal. The same is true of Islam. In India the Turkish nobility looked upon itself as *Ashraf* (noble) and dismissed the local converts as *Arzal* (Plebeian) and even *Mawali* (agent).

Yet another question on their mind was why Hindus were asking for the return of mandirs-turned-mosques when they were not returning their temples to Buddhists since, according to them, India was once wholly Buddhist. Fact is that India never went wholly Buddhist. Buddhism was basically an urban, mercantile, middle-class phenomenon. Rural India never went Buddhist; it continued to be Saivite, Vaishnavite or Tantrik. And in any case

all ceremonies connected with birth, marriage and death even in Buddhist families, were conducted by Brahmins.

Some people have very wrong notions about the Buddhist-Sanatani relationship. Some people even think that Buddhism was driven out of India. The fact is that Buddhism in its institutional framework failed society and, therefore, faded away. But Buddhist ideas that were found good and wholesome were adapted and adopted by Hindus. Vegetarianism is one of them. As a result, the Hindu of India is much more Buddhist than a Buddhist of Burma or Sri Lanka, China or Japan.

My friends in Aligarh thought that Afghanistan had prevailed against the Soviet Union because it is an Islamic country. So I put it to them: "How did Vietman stand up to USA? Was it Islam? Or even Buddhism? It was nationalism—love of your country, your people, your culture." In the case of Afghanistan there is the additional factor of geography which fosters the spirit of independence, as in Switzerland. It was this spirit that made Afghanistan resist Islamic invasions for three long centuries. Earlier, this same spirit made Afghanistan give a terrific fight to Alexander, so much so that the latter did not dare to return to his Greek home by the same Afghan route, but through Sindh and Baluchistan which, incidentally, also cost him dearly. And Afghanistan, at that time, was Buddhist!

A fundamental question the students raised was: Is not the *Ramayan* a myth and is not history superior to myth? I told them it is wrong to assume that history is superior to myth. While history is at best factual, myths embody the wisdom and morality of the ages. Whether the *Ramayana* is history or myth, or more myth than history, is not terribly important. The *Ramayana* even as pure literature, represents a people and reflects a civilization, a whole value-system. That is its importance. It is therefore, more important than all the so-called histories of ancient India put together. In any case, you never know where history ends and mythology begins. As Arnold Toynbee says in his *Study of History*, there is lot of history in myths and lot of myth in history.

□

Separateness, Yes; Separatism, No!

The Muslim can have a separate law but his heart must beat in unison with the Hindu heart.

—*Shri Guruji*

Everybody says that religion should not be mixed with politics. And then everybody goes and mixes his religion with his politics in the proportion of his choice, to his taste. Here is a clear case of double-think and double-talk.

Since difference of religion or sect has often marked combatants in war, religion has come to be considered a major factor in war-making. Actually there have not been many religious wars in history. And even so-called Religious Wars had more politics and economics, than religion, in them.

A second factor in the defamation of religion *vis-a-vis* politics, is the nature and position of religion in the West. Christianity being a credal dogmatic religion, it got very much discredited when scientific developments proved the untruth of many Christian beliefs and dogmas. On top of it the Church in Europe was identified with the Pope in Rome, who presumed to act as a legatee of the Roman Empire. European princes resented this situation, ran down the Pope and his works, and established their own national churches. These latter were more nationalist than religious in their orientation. And so, to this day, the monarch of England is "Defender of the Faith", and all its clergymen in the UK are paid by the state!

In India, the situation is entirely different. Hinduism being a naturalist, *'Sanatan' Dharma*, it does not stand on any dogmas which can be demolished by science. Indeed modern science often confirms Hindu religious insights into the nature of Reality. And in Hindu India, religion has never been the hand-maid of princes. *Dharma* here has stood as a sovereign principle of a just and moral life, above prince and pauper alike. However, our superficial politicians mouth 'secularism' as if it were some kind of a *mantra*, without understanding either *dharma* or science or history.

Fact is that our entire Freedom Movement was inspired by the religious impulse represented by Bharat Mata. It was spiritual leaders like Dayanand, Ramakrishna, Vivekanand and Aurobindo who laid the foundations of modern Indian national consciousness. Just listen to the historic *Uttarpara* speech of Sri Aurobindo: "This Hindu Nation was born with *Sanatan Dharma*; with it, it moves, it grows. When the *Sanatan Dharma* declines, then the Nation declines. The *Sanatan Dharma*, that is nationalism. This is the message that I have to speak to you." The appeal of Gandhi was entirely religious, moral. All his concepts—*Satya, Ahimsa, Satyagraha, Harijan, Brahmacharya, Ram Rajya* were moral concepts. His day began and ended with prayer and *Ramdhun*.

Anybody who conceives of India as a secular state, in the sense that it has no religious undertones or moral overtones, is dangerously ignorant of India and Indians, of Indian culture and Indian history. Such a sanitised, castrated state will have no root or branch. It will inspire neither affection nor loyalty; and it can only breed cynicism and corruption. An Indian State, if it is to be rooted in the affections of the people, must reflect their innermost thoughts. It must respond to the hopes, fears and aspirations of the people. The state must take on the spirit and flavour of the National Society at its best. Only a willing acceptance of Indian culture as the basis of the Indian State, will nourish the roots of society and strengthen the foundations of the state. Anything to the contrary will sap the foundations of the state, and will be rejected by any healthy society as foreign matter.

This does not mean that India should become a theocratic Hindu State in which non-Hindus will be second-class citizens.

Hinduism has never been a state religion. The only time in pre-Muslim times when there was an official state religion, was when Ashoka declared Buddhism the religion of the state. But in his own life-time, Ashoka's own ministers terminated that arrangement. When, therefore, the Hindu talks of a Hindu country, he is thinking of a cultural society; he is not thinking in terms of a state religion. Nor would he like any religious beliefs to be imposed on anyone. Freedom of religion is implicit in the Hindu way of life. (Let us not forget Muslims were living in peace and amity in Delhi even in 1192, and they fought on the side of Prithviraj, against Mohammed Ghori!) All that the Hindu wants is that Hindu values should be recognised, and Hindu *Sanskars* respected in Hindustan. A Sanskrit invocation with chanting of *Om*, or *puja* and *havan* with coconut and conchshell, should be welcomed as the right rituals for any solemn occasion in India to clear the atmosphere and uplift the soul.

People who oppose the above in the name of 'Secularism', forget three things. Firstly India is 85% Hindu—even as Egypt is about 85% Muslim—and democracy demands that their will should prevail. Secondly, the Hindu is *not* asking for a theological conformity; all he seeks is cultural unity and significance. And thirdly, the Hindu is apprehensive of the future. He sees mosques built over even historic temples like Ram Janmasthan Mandir in Ayodhya, Krishna Janmasthan Mandir in Mathura and Vishwanath Mandir in Kashi. He has seen the country partitioned before his eyes, in the name of Islam. And he sees Muslim population increasing disproportionately.

In this situation the Hindu feels insecure. Where even the majority society feels insecure, and is, therefore, jittery, you don't expect the minority to feel secure. It is essential for the security and satisfaction of majority and minority alike, that even while the principle of freedom of religion is recognised, the fact of the Hindu character of Hindustan is accepted without any reservations. Muslims must be free to pray the way they like, but they must live like Indians, and not as imitation Arabs or Iranians. They will do well to learn from Indonesians who are Muslim by religion but native Hindu by culture. They wisely see no contradiction in the

Ram at home and the Rahim in the mosque. Their Airline is called 'Garuda', and their dining tables are named after *Ramayana* heroes.

The Muslim Indian must remember the first lesson in civics; a man is free to play with his walking stick, but that freedom stops, where another person's nose begins. In India, Islam has to stop where Indian culture begins. The alternative would be a state within a state which can only disintegrate the state. Actually the trouble is not so much with the Muslim, who is only indulging an old habit, as with our governments, whose woolly-headed secularism is only a smokescreen for lack of character and loss of direction. And so even Jehovah's Witnesses, a freak Christian sect, presumes to oppose the singing of the National Anthem!

Very much more serious is the repeated 'official' visit of the Pope to India. Here is a religious leader presiding over a segment of the city of Rome. But his Vatican estate has been recognised as a 'State', with diplomatic representation in New Delhi! (At this rate we might as well have all our major *Muths* and *Ashrams* declared 'States'—with diplomatic status in other countries, and at the UN!) No wonder the Pope takes advantage of our stupidity and proposes to use his visit to 'save the souls' of our poor, by buying them for Christianity. Our people are used to so much nonsense in the name of secularism, that they think a little more nonsense will not do any great harm. And so they gulp it, albeit with 'patient deep disdain'.

Many Muslims have made much noise over the Supreme Court verdict, allowing maintenance to divorced Muslim women in the Shah Bano case. Privately they agree that the divorced Muslim women must be provided for. But they don't say, how. However, they are sure that any such maintenance allowance would be a violation of the Islamic law. For one thing, when 'religion' contradicts commonsense, it has to bow to it—or it will break. Secondly if the Muslim criminal law is dead and gone, why can't the Muslim civil law be at least improved upon? If Muslim law can be chopped and changed in Tunisia and Turkey, Algeria and Iran, why can't it be brought in line with developing concepts of justice, in India? If Pakistan can ban polygamy, why can't India do the same? Why does Hindu India have to be more Islamic than

even the 'Islamic Republic of Pakistan'?

A few weeks before he passed away, I saw Shri M.C. Chagla in Bombay. He said that Muslim Law was very progressive in its day, but that it had to be updated to modern standards of justice. He said that Government must go in for a Uniform Civil Law—and let the opponents of the same migrate to any land of their choice. He was sure no Muslim would take that option. The tragi-comedy of the Indian situation is that the Government which talks of the 21st century, is still mentally living in the 7th century!

The Muslim talks of his separate identity. No good Hindu will quarrel with that. The Hindu society itself has innumerable sub-identities within itself. That is why Shri Guruji Golwalkar of the RSS, while inaugurating the Deendayal Research Institute in New Delhi in 1972 said the Muslim could have his separate law, so long as his heart was one with the Hindu heart. However, what we have on our hands is a separate law *and* a separatist heart—and that means trouble.

There are identities and identities. The Muslim Indian is welcome to his separate religious identity. But he must have an Indian cultural identity, and not an Arab-Irani-Turkish cultural identity. A democratic separateness is alright, but a divisive separatism would be all wrong. As the great savant, Maulana Jalaluddin Rumi, put it in his *Masnavi* seven hundred years ago, *Hindian ra Hindi Istalah Madah*—the Hindis/Indians are welcome to the Hindi-Hindu-Indian idiom of life. Muslim Indians must own the Indian idiom of life—and not invoke foreign idiom in the name of Islam.

I repeat that the trouble is more with the Government than with Muslims or Christians. This government permits minorities to run their educational institutions with government aid but without government control. These institutions have the right to give minority religious instruction. But the common schools, which are, by definition, majority schools, have no right to give the majority Hindu religious-moral instruction. Gandhiji's word that every Hindu student must be taught Sanskrit and introduced to the *Gita*, is completely forgotten.

□

Hindus & Muslims: Blood Brothers

Ghoonghat ke patt khol re
Tohey piya milenge.

—*Kabir*

When India was partitioned, it was hoped that that would at least be the end of the Muslim problem. Today that problem is perceived to be still very much there. In addition to the old communal problem, we have the new Indo-Pak international problem. Only men of thought and feeling like poets, philosophers and saints, men who see life intensely and see it whole, men who take a mountain-top view of things—can see the problem in its totality and in its inwardness. Only they can help us solve this problem amicably, sensibly and finally.

We must clearly understand that we don't have Indian Muslims—that is, Muslims who happen to be living in India; what we have is Muslim Indians—Indians, who happen to be Muslim. Muslim Indians are infinitely nearer to Hindu Indians—in terms of race, language, culture, customs, habits—than to Muslims in Iran or Arabia. Not even 0.1 per cent of Muslim Indians can trace their ancestry to non-Indian origin; even though some of them might call themsleves *Qureshi, Durrani* and *Teherani*. Muslim Indians and Hindu Indians are blood brothers.

Hindus have an acute sense of grievance over 'Muslim' mayhem in India. This is very true—and very tragic. But there have been diverse tyrants—and innumerable victims of their tyranny. Christians in the middle ages could be as ruthless as Muslims;

and Arabs themselves were brutally attacked and subjugated by 'Muslim' Turks and Mongols.

Muslim Indians have a sense of loss of their glory of Mughal days. Fact is that 'Muslim' Indians had about as much share in this glory under 'Muslim' rule, as Indian Christians had under England's 'Christian' rule. Jaipur was more important, politically and militarily, for the Mughal, than all the five Bahmani 'Indian Muslim' states in the Deccan put together. While the king and his *subedars* ruled from the cities, the Hindu Rajas, *zamindars*, traders and clerks ruled the roost everywhere else. Muslim pockets were very much islands of Muslim influence in a sea of Hindu humanity. And these islands thought of themsleves as 'one' only under the influence of Wahabi Shah Waliallah after the collapse of Mughal empire.

Over the centuries, many Hindus embraced Islam—as a result of force or temptation. That state power was not the only factor in conversions, is proved by the fact that U.P., where Muslims ruled the longest, has a huge Hindu majority, but East Bengal, where they ruled for much less time, the Hindus are in a minority. However, even in their new faith, Muslims retained many of the attitudes and institutions of the old, complete with the ideas of right and wrong and high and low, of amulets and *Pirs* in life, and of *chadars* and lamps in death. And so, for example, for Shaikh Nizamuddin Aulia of Delhi, "a command of the *Pir* (*Guru*) is like a command of the Prophet", and a visit to the *Pir's* tomb is "spiritually more exhilarating than a pilgrimage to Mecca."

Islam prescribes burial underground—and not even a grave above it. But Muslims in India have built palatial tombs over the dead, including 'Taj Mahal'! Similarly, Arabs know nothing about *Tazias*. In India, *Tazias* were developed in imitation of the *Rath Yatra* of Puri Jagannath! Aurangzeb had even banned *Tazias* as 'un-Islamic'! He had banned music too—but today Muslims are not only some of the best singers, they may even sing of Krishna! And even *Dargahs* resound with music!

Kings fought each other; and they even invoked religion—to excite people to fight and kill. But these wars were basically struggles for power—and not for religion. In any case Humayun Kabir noted, there were more wars between Muslims and Muslims than between Hindus and Muslims. Kings and their agents slaughtered people; but people as such, Hindus and Muslims, did not go about stabbing each other. Hindu-Muslim 'riots' are basically a phenomenon of the British period.

Ruler after Muslim ruler gave preferential treatment to Muslims. But they also gave special concessions to 'Multanis', Hindu traders, in the interest of the economy. The big empire led to a huge common market and increased trade. There were regular camel *caravans* from Banaras to Baghdad.

Even under Muslim rule there were innumerable rich Hindu traders, and Mughal kings often borrowed money from them. While the *kazis* sided with the kings in orthodoxy, the Sufi saints criticised both, the kings and the *kazis*, for their corruption and their hypocrisy. And it is these Sufi saints who set the tone for Muslim masses.

Out of evil came some great good. Delhi suppressed Sanskrit and imposed Persian on India. But Persian could never become the people's language. And so all our regional languages had an opportunity to come up and flower forth! The need to resist and fight the tyrant, necessitated the emergence of "warrior-gods", and Rama and Krishna now for the first time became the two most important incarnations in India! They were almost unknown to Chandragupta Maurya and Ashoka.

Babar, the very first Mughal ruler, banned cow slaughter and this ban continued until the British took over. Just like the old Hindu Kings, the Mughals drank only *Ganga-Jal*, wherever they were. Akbar and his successors right down to Bahadur Shah—including Aurangzeb—were not circumcised. Just like the Hindu rulers of old, they gave in charity their weight (*Tulya-daan*) in gold, etc. And they gave the morning *Jharokha Darshan* to the public—another old Indian royal practice—to reassure the public that they were alive and well! By blood, Jahangir was half-Hindu—and Shah Jahan was three-fourths Hindu. They called themselves *Jahangir* (Keeper of the World) and *Shah Jahan* (World Ruler), to the intense

irritation of the Khalifa and the Turks. Aurangzeb removed the *Kalma* from his coins—on the ground that the Hindus were also touching them! Akbar banned Haj because of its hazards and he made it clear that "India cannot be ruled by Arab rules of a thousand years ago"!

Aurangzeb was a violent fanatic. But even he was more of a king than a *momin*. He did not so much as bother about the Khalifa in Turkey. He neither informed him of his ascension to the throne nor asked for his recognition or blessings. Indeed the Mughal rulers regarded themselves as Khalifas—and some of them thought they were prophets!

Aurangzeb fought to keep Central Asia attached to Delhi. He made the revealing remark that while other Indian princes fought for their respective principalities, he was the only one to think of "All India"! Here was Indian national interest, at the core of the Mughal empire.

While the Hindu saints rejected fanaticism and resisted tyranny, they had nothing against Islam as such. Tukaram said: "Never forget to take the name of Allah first!" Even immigrant Muslims developed intense love for India. For Amir Khusru, "Delhi people are like angels." "Mecca", he said, "should go round Delhi in reverence...Compared to India the rest of the world is a prison."

Particularly after the death of Aurangzeb in 1707, and until the armed uprising in 1857, Hindus and Muslims increasingly lived in peace and amity as 'Hindustanis'. It was the British who sabotaged this unity by favouring now one community and now another. It was they who, after 1857, destroyed the psychological unity of the Indian Army by re-organising it on caste and community lines. Until 1857, Hindus and Muslims served together in the same Army units.

The popular impression that Muslims were pro-British, is only a half-truth. Muslims, if anything, resented British power even more than the Hindus. Tipu Sultan was the only Indian ruler who died fighting the British. And Muslims resisted even British culture and English language much more than the Hindus. For all these reasons, for a long time, the British were more anti-Muslim than anti-Hindu. The Muslims took a much more active part in the 1857 uprising than the Hindus. After 1857, the British cursed every Muslim rebel as *Badmash* (rogue) while the Hindu rebel was only dismissed as a 'Pandey' (after the first rebel, Mangal Pandey). It was only after 1905, when the Hindus began to talk of *Swarajya*, and to practise *Swadeshi*, that the British became anti-Hindu and pro-Muslim—and the Muslim became increasingly pro-British. Even then, in the 1921 movement, the Muslim was more active than the Hindu.

That being the historic perspective, it should be possible for Hindus and Muslims to resolve their problems amicably and finally—on the basis of good sense and good faith. Unfortunately, a bad communal situation, inherited from the British, has been further worsened by the Congress. Although Congress has been in power since 1947, it says that Muslims are not getting their due—as though somebody other than itself is responsible for it, assuming the allegation to be correct. Even when there are big riots, either there is no inquiry—or the report is not published. Nobody is ever punished. And compensation itself tends to be political. One would suspect Congress has a vested interest in riots—so that it can pose as the protector of Muslims. The 1986 Meerut riots were purely political. The Bofors scandal was proving too much of an embarrassment and so policemen were sent to shoot Muslims to divert attention away from corruption, and towards 'communalism'.

Some short-sighted Muslims have also been stoking communal fires by now refusing to sing *Vande Matram* and then opposing a Uniform Civil Law—and generally complaining all the time.

In this situation it is for men of vision and wisdom to look beyond the Present, into the Past and the Future—for a lasting solution of this problem on the basis of Facts and Justice.

1. First of all the history of India, written by the British from the imperial angle, and mechanically regurgitated ever since by Indian authors, should be replaced by one written by Indians from the Indian angle. Such a history should be polycentric and not Delhi-centric. It should be people-oriented and not king-centred.

It should not suppress unpleasant facts; but it should not overlook pleasant facts. Such a factual, positive and balanced history of the Indian people, re-educating the Indian mind, will do more to harmonise relations than anything else.

2. The life, limb, property and honour of all citizens must be safe. District officers must be held fully responsible for law and order. If, even then, there is violence, it must be inquired into. The findings of such inquiries must be made public—the guilty punished, and the victims compensated.

3. An impotent Minorities Commission does no good to anybody. It irritates the Hindus but does not serve the Muslims. Now that we have a National Human Rights Commission, the MC should go—and we should have NHRC even at provincial and district levels, to deal with all complaints of discrimination on grounds of caste, creed or language. That will serve and please—both, Hindus and Muslims.

4. Hindus have a deep sense of grievance over the excesses of invaders, who happened to be Muslim. Muslim Indians should look upon these scourages of humanity as invaders, and not as "fellow-Muslims". (Muslims in Sindh, Pakistan, have already shown the way by acclaiming Raja Dahir Sen, the last Hindu ruler of Sindh, as a great hero, and Mohammed-Bin-Qasim, as invader and enslaver.) By way of a goodwill gesture, Muslim Indians should return to Hindu Indians, the three more important temples, known to have been forcibly converted into mosques by tyrannical kings.

5. Muslim Indians should not try to be more Muslim than even the Mughals; they should heartily celebrate Dussehra and Diwali, Basant and Holi, etc. And Hindus should not hesitate to associate with the celebration of Id, Moharrum etc., in mixed localities, as they used to do until only sixty years ago. If non-Christians can exchange gifts and greetings on Christmas, why can't Hindu and Muslim friends do the same on Id and Diwali?

6. Urdu is seventy-five per cent Hindi. And so, even as Braj, Avadhi, Bhojpuri, Maithili, Rajasthani etc., are accepted as forms of 'Hindi', such Urdu works, as are *not* highly Persianised—and,

therefore, are easily understood—should be included in Hindi courses in school and college. This should be in addition to the prevailing position of Urdu in Persian script.

7. If Muslims are not yet ready for Uniform Civil Law they should at least accept the Family Laws as amended by Pakistan. Accordingly, polygamy should be banned in India, as it is already banned in Pakistan and several other Muslim countries. This will protect Muslim womanhood and allay Hindu fears of disproportionate increase of Muslim population, allegedly because of polygamy.

8. Muslim Members of the Constituent Assembly had urged Proportional Representation in the Indian legislatures, for a proper representation of all sections of the population. Muslims leaders still feel strongly about it. And they are right; outside of Anglo-America, most of the democratic countries have the system of proportional representation. Indian Electoral Law could also be reformed accordingly—to give proper representation to all minorities—religious, lingual and political.

9. Indians—Hindu and Muslim—should help each other wherever they can. For example Muslim Indians wishing to visit Pakistan, and Muslim Pakistanis wishing to visit India, should be given passports and visas, respectively, without much ado. Indeed the goal should be to allow free movement of men, materials and ideas all over the 'Hindustan Peninsula'.

Likewise Muslims should try to help Hindus living in Muslim countries. For example Hindus working in Arab countries are not allowed to build temples. A Hindu dying in some of these countries, cannot be cremated—or even buried—there. This makes for much inconvenience. Muslim Indians should plead the case of Hindu Indians on these issues. It is possible that Arab countries will take their own time to do the needful; but Muslim Indians should do their duty by their Hindu brethren. Gestures like these generate great goodwill.

10. And above all Hindus and Muslims must learn to respect each other's religious leaders. As Gandhiji had rightly put it: "There is in Hinduism room enough for Jesus, as there is for Mohammed,

Zoroaster and Moses." Hindus should not hesitate to respect Mohammed as a great man, even as they admire a Lenin or a Napoleon. For whatever else he was or was not, Mohammed was certainly the greatest Arab leader in history. Likewise Muslim Indians should not hesitate to adore Rama and Krishna. Let them remember that Muslim Iran prides itself on its pre-Islamic heroes like Rustom and Sohrab; Muslim Egypt glories in pre-Islamic Pharoahs Rameses and Cleopatra; and Muslim Indonesia has Sri Rama as its National Hero No. 1.

If Hindus and Muslims ponder these matters calmly, and respond to these suggestions positively, the ground could be prepared for a Great Reconciliation in the Hindustan Peninsula. It will be a great day for our long-suffering humanity. It will be a great day for all mankind.

Kabir beckons us—

Ghoonghat ke patt khol re,
Tohey Piya milenge.

(Lift the veil—and you will see the beloved.)

The Muslim problem is old; but it is not insoluble. If there is the will, there will be a way. Let all men of goodwill think and work in this direction.

□

Imam of Mecca on Ayodhya

If archaeological and historical facts prove that the Babri Mosque was built after demolishing a Hindu temple, the Indian Muslims should hand over the complex to the Hindus and Muslims must avoid bloodshed in this connection. The issues of Babri Mosque and Al-Aqsa mosque are different. The latter was occupied by the Jews forcibly and the Muslims were evicted.

—*Imam of Mecca Mosque*

Imam of Haram-e-Sharif (mosque of Mecca) quoted in 'Observer of Business and Politics', New Delhi, Nov. 15, 1997

December 6, 1992

What is happening in India is a new historic awakening.

—V.S. Naipaul

During centuries of Turkish invasions and gross misrule, thousands of temples were desecrated and destroyed or converted into mosques. This left a deep wound on the psyche of the Indian people. As Gujral told Pakistan Foreign Minister Yaqub: "Don't forget, Minister, that every Indian carries on his shoulder the burden of a thousand years of history" (*vide* Iqbal Ahmad's 'Benazir'). The Government of independent India recognised this fact and the Nehru Cabinet in 1947 promptly okayed the reconstruction of Somnath Temple destroyed by Mahmud Ghazni. Unfortunately it overlooked the demands for the restoration of Rama Janmasthan Mandir in Ayodhya, Krishna Janmasthan Mandir in Mathura and Kashi Vishwanath Mandir in Varanasi.

In the Eighties the Vishwa Hindu Parishad reminded the country that Hindu-Muslim relations would improve only when historic wrongs were righted, however symbolically. Arnold Toynbee, the great historian, in his Azad Memorial Lectures in Delhi in 1960 pointed out that early in the 19th century, Russia had occupied much of Poland and built a Russian Orthodox Church in the heart of Roman Catholic Warsaw, capital of Poland. "The Russians had done this to give the Poles a continuous ocular demonstration that the Russians were now their masters."

When after World War I, Poland became free, it promptly

pulled down the Russian Church. Said Toynbee: "I do not greatly blame the Polish government for having pulled down that Russian Church. The purpose for which the Russians had built it had been not religious but political and the purpose had also been intentionally offensive."

Toynbee then referred to the Muslim conversion of temples in Varanasi and elsewhere into mosques and said that while he appreciated the government's efforts to preserve them, "perhaps the Poles were really kinder in destroying the Russians' self-discrediting monument in Warsaw than you have been in sparing Aurangzeb's mosques."

Instead of conceding the reasonable VHP demand, a whole string of governments of India began playing politics with it. The locks on the disputed structure were removed by court orders in 1986. The foundation stone for Ram Janmasthan Mandir was laid in 1988. In January 1989, the Rajiv government drafted a Memorandum of Understanding for shifting the "super-structure of the building known as Babri Masjid from its present site at Shri Ram Janmabhoomi at Ayodhya to a suitable site near the *Mazar* of Mir Baqi in Sahanwa village in the district of Faizabad". The Archaeological Survey of India duly prepared a detailed plan to shift the structure, stone by stone, and put it together at the new site. The VHP signed this MoU. But Muslim leaders failed to do so. And the PM looked helplessly on.

Mr. V.P. Singh, the next PM, told the VHP; *Arre Bhai Masjid hi kyon kahte ho* (But why do you refer to it as a mosque at all?) *Woh to Ram Lalla Ka Mandir hi hai* (That is just the temple of the Baby Ram). *Demolition ki zarroorat hi kahaan hai Bhai* (where is the need for demolition). *Ek dhakka doge to woh gir jayega* (one shove and it will crumble) (*vide The National Herald*, October 30, 1990). But he issued an Ordinance, only to withdraw it under communal pressure within 48 hours.

Chandra Shekhar as Prime Minister only wanted to know whether a Hindu structure had stood on the Ayodhya site before—so that he could lawfully restore it to Hindus. However, he was out before he could proceed in the matter. The next PM, P.V.

Narasimha Rao, commissioned Chandraswami to try and divide the Hindu religious leaders. He kept the Damocles' sword of Article 356 hanging over the head of the BJP government in U.P. And he rushed 16,000 troops to Ayodhya, which only hotted up the atmosphere. The result was December 6.

The Sangh Parivar wanted the structure shifted legally, in an orderly manner; they never wanted it pulled down the way it was. Who did it? Obviously people who wanted to give BJP a bad name and to have the four BJP State Governments dismissed.

On December 1, 1992, Arjun Singh, then senior Cabinet minister, sent 'a source report about events in Ayodhya' as also 'a copy of Fax message sent by an active Congress worker', to the Cabinet Secretary. This letter said that if *karsevaks* did not demolish the structure, "some agent provocateurs from Pakistan have been able to infiltrate into Ayodhya and would try to damage the Babri Masjid." According to Saeed Naqvi, veteran journalist, there was celebration in the Pakistan High Commission in New Delhi on the evening of December 6. Our information is that on December 10, Congress leader Antulay sent a Marathi Fax message to Mr. Narasimha Rao saying that the RSS was not at fault and that members of his own kitchen Cabinet were involved in the demolition. In a TV chat earlier this year, S.B. Chavan, then home minister, also held Mr. Rao responsible for December 6.

These are the facts. But the people who demanded the partition of India or supported that demand, or acquiesced in that demand, and who aided and abetted communalism to corner that vote bank, condemn the Sangh Parivar as 'communal'. It is like the pot calling the kettle black.

While everybody regretted the disorderly manner of Dec. 6, Nirad Chaudhuri said: "Muslims do not have the slightest right to complain about destruction of one mosque. From 1000 AD every Hindu temple from Kathiawar to Bihar from the Himalaya to the Vindhyas has been sacked and ruined... No nation with any self-respect will forgive this." And V.S. Naipaul said: "In Ayodhya the construction of a mosque on a spot regarded as sacred by the conquered population was meant as an insult." About December 6 he

said: "What is happening in India is a new, historical awakening... Today it seems to me that Indians are becoming alive to their history...What is happening in India is a mighty creative process."

The people of India agree. They keep voting more and more for BJP. More and more Muslims are also beginning to see BJP as the party which thinks straight, talks straight, acts straight on the principle: 'Justice for all: appeasement of none.' The unofficial thinking in the Home Ministry in 1992-93 also was that the Hindu-Muslim problem was more or less solved on December 6. It is significant that, after December 6 and the Bombay serial blasts, there has been virtually no communal violence in the country. Out of evil cometh good. *Satyameva Jayate*.

Naipaul on Ayodhya

The people who say that there was no temple there (Ayodhya) are missing the point. Babar, you must understand, had contempt for the country he had conquered. And his building of that mosque was an act of contempt for the country.

One needs to understand the passion that took them (*Karsevaks*) on top of the domes. The jeans and the tee-shirts are superficial. The passion alone is real. You can't dismiss it. You have to try to harness it....

What is happening in India is a new, historical awakening, a mighty creative process. Indian intellectuals, who want to be secure in their liberal beliefs, may not understand what is going on, especially if these intellectuals happen to be in the United States. But every other Indian knows that a larger response is emerging even if at times this response appears in his eyes to be threatening....

I don't see the Hindu reaction purely in terms of one fundamentalism pitted against another. The reaction is a much larger response.....the sense of history that the Hindus are now developing is a new thing.

–Naipaul interview to Dilip Padgaonkar
'The Times of India', July 18, 1993

Who Demolished the Disputed Structure?

Masjid dha de, mandir dha de;
Dha de jo kuchh dhainda
Ek bande da dil na dhaheen
Sohna Rab dilan vich rahenda.

December 6, 1992 was a Sunday. Normally, on Sundays, BJP seniors do not visit 11 Ashoka Road, the party headquarters in Delhi. There is no press briefing. But since *kar seva* on a huge scale was scheduled for that day some of us decided to be around.

On the morning of December 6, I saw *Sarvashri* Bhandari, Kushabhau, Kedarnath and Ashwini there. Bhandariji had been just back from Ayodhya. He told us about the arrangements and the programme in Ayodhya for the day. I then retired to draft a press release on the basis of Bhandariji's account.

I was still at it when Ashwiniji came and told me that the release would not be needed and went away. I could not make head or tail of it and so I went in to see what was the matter. They were all sitting stunned. Sunderlal Patwa had just rung up to say that the CBI had told the State Government that the Ayodhya structure was being pulled down and that Shiv Sainiks were believed to have done it. (The fact is that many trains, including the one carrying the Shiv Sainiks, had been stalled at Jhansi, Kanpur etc., because there was just no room in Ayodhya for fresh arrivals).

That afternoon Bhandariji and myself met the press. We said

that what had happened was most 'unfortunate'. The BJP, we said, had endorsed the VHP demand for restoration of the ancient sacred sites in Kashi, Mathura and Ayodhya. But we had urged the respectful shifting of the structure stone by stone (for instance, to the *Mazar* of Mir Baqi at Sahanwa village in district Faizabad) as had been done in Egypt to save ancient temples from the Aswan Dam waters. And the Archaeological Department had prepared a plan for the purpose. Demolition of a religious structure, even if disputed, went against the Indian grain.

Aitzaz Ashan, Pakistani leader, quotes a Punjabi verse in his book *The Indus Saga*:

Masjid dha de, mandir dha de, Dha de jo kuchh dhainda;
Ek bande da dil na dhaheen, Sohna Rab dilan vich rahenda

(You may demolish any mosque or temple, but do not hurt the heart of any man, for God lives in our hearts.)

And December 6, 1992, had hurt many hearts.

We in the Sangh Parivar knew we had not done it. But we did not know who had done it. So we kept silent.

Our opponents, and even the common man, could always say that we had wanted it gone, and we were there in huge numbers, so who else could have done it? We suffered this indignity in silence.

Eye-witnesses have told me that leaders were addressing lakhs of *karsevaks* out of sight, some furlongs away. Only a few thousand of them were standing by for formal *karseva*, when about a hundred young men wearing a different head-band—and reportedly staying in a Faizabad hotel—tried to break the cordon of the police and *Swayamsevaks*. They were thrown back. A second attempt by them was also repulsed. And then a couple of persons were seen on top of the dome. That changed the mood of some onlookers. The rest, as they say, is history.

Shrikant Joshi, the private secretary of the then RSS *Sarsanghchalak*, Balasaheb Deoras, told the press that there was reason to believe that the dastardly deed had been done by RAW. Two years back, former RSS *Sarsanghchalak* Rajju Bhaiya said that some *karsevaks* had lost their cool and started removing the plaster when the mayhem broke out.

Sudarshanji has said—on the basis of a Nirmala Deshpande interview—that there was probably a bomb explosion. He has also referred to the dubious activities of Narasimha Rao's kitchen Cabinet. Nirmalaji has said that she knew who had done it but their names would be made public only after her death. She has also said that the top BJP leadership had nothing to do with the demolition but some lesser partymen had hired experts for the purpose.

All these bits of information could be true. There is no contradiction between them. A heavy dome falling with a huge thud could sound like an explosion. The important thing is to go deep into the matter and find out all the relevant facts.

Soon after December 6, the press had published a photograph—again recently reproduced—of Murli Manohar Joshi and Uma Bharti in excited joy on the occasion. This does not indicate complicity but a mixture of surprise and joy. Such a response has been described by Aristotle as 'catharsis'—the purging of the effects of pent-up emotions and repressed thoughts. In a cathartic situation, the heart is bursting with contrary emotions and a person may laugh or cry—or do both, laugh and cry—and emerge the purer in the process.

In criminal investigations, the rule is to see who stood to profit by the crime. And in the present case the needle of suspicion points unmistakably to the Rao Government. The BJP was becoming a serious challenge to the Congress. The demolition could be used to give the BJP a bad name. It could be used to dismiss the four BJP-led State Governments. And it would take away from the BJP a standing issue. The Muslim leadership agreed.

Rao tried to confound the RSS, VHP and BJP. He had promised in July 1992 to solve the problem within three months and he had assured that there would be a court judgement by October 12. (It came on December 11, two months too late.) And in the 18 days preceding December 6, Rao had not contacted or consulted L.K. Advani, leader of the Opposition, even once. Obviously, he had decided on action—on a showdown.

On December 6, the State Government was more dead than alive. And Rao in his wisdom had positioned over 16,000 soldiers

in Ayodhya. What were they doing? Did they question men openly carrying heavy ropes, pick axes and other tools? Was even a single person detained? No wonder even his friend S.B. Chavan, then Home Minister, holds him responsible for December 6.

Although Rao has much to answer for, his role would not constitute the whole truth behind December 6. In the last few years we have suffered several surprising shocks. Who, for example, stood behind the blowing up of *Kanishka*? Who masterminded the midnight air-dropping of weaponry in Purulia in December 1995? The Bombay serial blasts was an act of war. It was supposed to be the 'Muslim' reaction to December 6. Is it a fact that RDX consignments had been landed in India even before December 6? Was there a link between all these mysterious goings on?

In his book '*Will Pakistan Break Up*'? Muneer Ahmed of Pakistan writes that in July 1993, Pakistani President Ghulam Ishaq Khan told Nawaz Sharief: "The ISI is behind these (Bombay) blasts and I have got proof of it." He also told him that if the US declares Pakistan a terrorist State as a result of these ISI activities, he would hold him responsible. The question is: Who controls ISI? The Pakistan Government or somebody else?

Did RAW have a finger in this bloody pie, as alleged in 1992? In 1996, the number two man in the Intelligence Bureau, Rattan Sehgal, was found having serious unauthorised relations with the CIA. Did the IB and/or its friends have a role in the events of December 6?

The BJP does not have to accuse the Congress of unlocking the disputed structure. And Congress does not have to accuse BJP of demolishing the structure. We must know all the facts and not just go about bandying charges and filing fancy cases. December 6 was much too serious for that kind of frivolity.

Perhaps the Government could seize and seal all files, films and tapes on the Ayodhya issue—from the day of the unlocking. These files could be submitted to a commission of three retired Supreme Court judges. And this commission could give its findings within one year. Let the country know the truth, the whole truth and nothing but the truth.

□

VII. CULTURE

1. National Flag and National Anthem
2. Five Questions to the Pope
3. Manu Maharaj Ki Jai!
4. Rath Yatra....Tazia....Ganeshotsav
5. Jai Mata Di!

National Flag and National Anthem

When the Congress Flag Committee recommended Saffron Flag as National Flag.

A few years back after the regular Press Briefing, I remarked by way of *obiter dicta* that India will come into its own when the historic *Bhagwa Dhwaj* flies on the Red Fort and an appropriate verse from the Vedas is adopted as National Anthem. The opinion was unorthodox. And some friends commented upon it in their writings.

Obviously this was not, and is not, BJP policy. And it can materialise only if, as and when the Parliament wants it. Incidentally, Piloo Modi used to say, it is the most distinctive flag. It is the colour of the glorious dawn!

It is not widely known that the Karachi session of Congress appointed a Flag Committee to finalise a National Flag, since a variety of tricolours had been used over the decades. This Committee consisted of Sardar Patel (President), Maulana Azad, Pandit Nehru, Master Tara Singh, Kaka Kalelkar, Dr. Hardikar and Pattabhi Sitaramayya (Convener). Its unanimous report was that "The National Flag should be a *Kesari* or Saffron colour, having on it at the left top quarter the *Charkha* in blue", since that colour is 'non-communal' and "is associated with this ancient country by long tradition" (*vide* File No. 11/27-1927, Important Pamphlets and Schemes 79-F, Nehru Memorial Museum and Library, Teen Murti House, New Delhi). It is a mystery why this unanimous report of the Flag Committee was never implemented.

Many Muslim brethren think *Bhagwa Dhwaja* to be 'Hindu'. It is not 'Hindu' in the sense of being non-Muslim. It is ancient Indian. Many Muslims think that Green is the Flag of Islam. It is not. Green was the flag of the Turkish Empire. As for Prophet Mohmmed is concerned, the late Dr. Saifuddin Jeelani, Arab scholar and journalist of Calcutta, said that the Prophet had carried flags of many shades in his many wars—including on one occasion, saffron—but, it so happens, that he had never carried a green flag. If, as and when, therefore, the Indian Parliament decides on a Saffron Flag, Muslims should welcome it as heartily as anybody else.

The same is with National Anthem. During the Freedom Movement the anthem was *Vande Mataram*. After Independence, it was *Jana Gana Mana*. Shri Guruji used to say that *Vande Mataram* had been by-passed because of Muslim objection and *Jana Gana Mana* seems to have been preferred because of its musical proximity to 'God Save the King'. That's okay. But perhaps it would have been best to pick up one from the *Vedas* or the epics. They are so rich in noble sentiments.

We have all heard of Rama telling Lakshman:

Api Swarnamayi Lanka
na mi Laxmana rochate,
Janani Janmabhoomishcha
Swargadapi gariyasi.

"Oh Laxmana, even the golden Lanka has no fascination for me. For the Mother and the Motherland are greater than heaven itself."

And the *Mahabharata* says:

Atrapi Bharatam shrestham
Jambudweepe mahamune,
Yato hi Karmabhooresha
Yatonya bhogabhoomayah.
Atra janma sahasranam
Sahasrairapi sattama,
Kadachillabhate jantur
Manushyam punyasanchayat.

"Bharat is the greatest land on earth, and it alone is the land of action while the rest are lands of pleasure. It is only after great acquisition of merit that a person gets the privilege of being born a human being in this country."

Even the *Atharva Veda* says:

Mata bhoomih putroham prithivyah.

"This land is the mother and I am her son."

It goes on to say:

Janam bibhrati bahudha vivachasam
nana dharmanam prithivi yathoukasam.

"This our Motherland gives equal shelter to people speaking different languages and following different faiths."

It even says: "*Yo no dweshat prithivi yah pritanyat Yobhidasat manasa yo wadhena*

Tam no bhoome randhaya purvakritwari.

"Oh Motherland, those who hate us, those who assault us with armies, those who desire to enslave and to destroy us—may all these be destroyed."

Thc *Rig Veda* says:

Aa yad vamiyachakshasa
mitra vayam cha surayah,
Vyachishte bahupayye
yatemahi Swarayie.

"Oh people with a wide outlook and a friendly attitude, let us all thinkers come together and endeavour for public good in a far-flung and well-protected *Swarajya*."

It adds:

Sangachchadhwam samvadadhwam
sam vo mansi jayatam.

Samani vo akuti samana hridayani vah. "Let us move together, let us speak together, let our minds think together and let our hearts feel together."

And it concludes:

Gayanti dewah kila geetakani
dhanyastu ye Bharatbhoomi-bhage.

"Even the gods are blessed when they get the privilege to

sing in Bharat!"

What other society has noble sentiments like these—and as old as the hills?

It is about time every Indian took pride in our country and our culture. This pride should not be confined to those who are 'Hindu' by religion. It must also be shared by those who are Hindu or Hindi by culture, though not by religious persuasion. For it is the common heritage of all of us from the Himalaya to the seas. All misunderstanding of, and allergy to, our ancient cultural heritage must cease. We must strengthen our roots—not weaken them.

□

India is Unique

In the morning I bathe my intellect in the stupendous and cosmological philosophy of the Bhagwat Gita. The pure Walden Water is mingled with the sacred water of the Ganges.

—Henry David Thoreau

The real antithesis is not between East and West but between India and the rest of the world.

—Dickinson

Aurobindo: "Dickinson is right."

—'Father India' by Jeffery Paine

Sarmad tera duniya mein bada naam hua;
Jab Kufr se tu maele Islam hua;
Allah wa Nabi mein burai kya thi
Kyon phir ke murid-e-Lachhman wa Ram hua?

—Sufi Poet Saint Martyr Sarmad

("Sarmad, you got much name and fame when you switched from Kuffr [Judaism] to Islam. But what was wrong with Allah and the Prophet that you have now become a disciple of Rama and Lakshmana?")

Five Questions to the Pope

Janam bibhrati bahuda vivachasam
Nana dharmanam prithvi Yathoukasam.

—*Atharva Veda*

Some time back the United States launched an attack on the Bharatiya Janata Party (BJP), its ideological mentor, the Rashtriya Swayamsevak Sangh (RSS), and "other Hindu organisations" for their opposition to religious conversions. The attack came in a global survey on religious freedom conducted by the US State Department and mandated by the US Congress.

The US even suggested that Robert Seiple, its Ambassador at Large, who runs its International Religious Freedom Office in the State Department, visit India and study the problem on the spot.

The Government of India only gave expression to strong Indian public opinion on the subject when it immediately made it clear to Washington that Seiple would not be welcome. Washington's ignorance of the Indian scene and its insensitivity to Indian feelings seem to be truly appalling.

India has always been the land of religious freedom. The *Atharva Veda* says:

"*Janam, bibhrati bahuda vivachasam,*
Nana dharmanam prithvi Yathoukasam."

(This our motherland gives equal shelter to people speaking different languages and following different faiths).

Christianity came to India long before it went to Europe. We have had Syrian Christians as an integral and harmonious part of Indian society for over 1,500 years. But India has always resented conversions effected by the Portuguese by force and, by the British, through state patronage. All self-respecting Indians resented Bishop Heber's lines that, in India,

"Every prospect pleases
And man alone is vile"

—just because the man is Hindu, and not convert to Christianity.

Swami Vivekanand, the hero of the Parliament of Religions in Chicago, 1893, said: "If all India stands up and takes all the mud at the bottom of the Indian Ocean and throws it up against the Western countries, it will not be doing an infinitesimal part of that which you are doing to us." He added: "But they dare not do that to the Mohammedans of India; the sword will be out."

Mahatma Gandhi had said: "It is not unusual to find Christianity synonymous with denationalisation." He had added: "If I had the power, and could legislate, I would certainly stop all proselytisation." He looked forward to converts returning to their ancestral faith. He had described it as *Ghar Vapasi* (home-coming).

The Constituent Assembly of India, in its innocence, gave citizens the freedom to preach and propagate religion. But churches, supported by the wealth of Western countries, have been busy converting poor Indian tribal people by the million, and in the process eroding their tribal culture and subverting their loyalty to India.

Chief Justice Neogi of the Nagpur High Court, inquiring into the activities of foreign missionaries in Central India, reported in 1956 "an unholy alliance between Roman Catholics and American money in India." And Verrier Elvin, a missionary who worked among tribal people, revealed that the Church has "an extensive money-lending business, and this is one of the most effective means of bringing aboriginals under their control and forcing them into the church." Jagjivan Ram, a leader of the 'lower' castes, warned that if conversions were not checked, in the years to come converts would demand a separate, sovereign Christian state.

It was in this light that a full bench of the Supreme Court ruled on January 7, 1977, that there was no fundamental right to convert and that conversions would impinge on freedom of conscience and disturb public order.

What has been happening in Gujarat, Madhya Pradesh, Orissa and now Bihar, between Hindus and Christians, is basically disturbance of order. The irony is that the disturbers are blaming the disturbed. And the Christian West has been using its media monopoly to defame India and Hindus. Even US President Bill Clinton and the Pope descended to this level.

The fact is that the Jhabua nuns rape case, in the Congress-ruled Madhya Pradesh, took place in a Christian village. In Gujarat, only one life was lost—and the victim was Navghan Vasava, a Hindu tribesman.

The burning of Australian missionary Graham Staines and his two sons in Orissa was certainly a case of criminal lunacy. But the Church seems to treat it as a case of "the blood of the martyrs becoming the seed of the Church."

However, there are many disturbing aspects to the unfortunate incident. Although the Church and the Congress were quick to blame Bajrang Dal, Justice Wadhwa of the Supreme Court, probing the matter, has found that the police complaint had been "doctored." Who was interested in doctoring it?

People are also asking why the leprosy expert was operating in an area not known for leprosy. They are also asking whether the missionary was engaged in converting poor tribes people, encouraging them to eat beef and defy tribal customs and traditions.

In the wake of this tragic incident, even the anti-BJP Congress Chief Minister, a Hindu, was replaced by a Christian. Even so, the Orissa Police was not able to nab the alleged killer Dara Singh for a whole year. Obviously, the main accused was able to hide even though he carried a price of $20,000 on his head, because he was popular with the tribespeople for his opposition to Church activities.

Nor is Dara Singh alone in Indian allergy to missionary activities. Even Inderjit Gupta, Home Minister in the Deve Gowda

and Gujral governments, has said the church is spreading separatism and terrorism in the Northeast. Jammu and Kashmir Chief Minister Farooq Abdullah and Defence Minister George Fernandes have said that Western propaganda on the Christian issue was a plot to defame and destabilize the government.

The Pope recently visited India unlike China which vetoed his visit, the Pope, was welcomed in India. But he needs to address questions in every good Indian heart.

The first: India is more religious than any other country in the world. Morally, it is more Christian than any Christian country. In this situation, does not exporting Christianity to India amount to carrying coals to New Castle? Is it not an insult to India to tell Hindus that they are all sinners and that only Jesus can save them?

Secondly: The Pope looks upon Protestant Churches trying to evangelize Roman Catholics in Brazil as "wolves." Would not Indians be right in looking at foreign missionaries with foreign money in India as super-wolves?

Third: When Indian men of religion go West, they go empty-handed, with only religion in their hearts. They succeed or fail on the merit of their message. But foreign missionaries here bring foreign money. In the words of Gandhi, they win "rice Christians" on the strength of their money.

An Indian, after studying various religions, and coming to the conclusion that Christianity is best for him, is welcome to convert. But is it fair to indulge in mass conversion of poor people by offering them financial advantage? Is not the Church acting as a junior partner of Western imperialism, including Western multi-national corporations?

Finally, there is a Roman Church in Western Europe. England has its own church. Russia has the Russian Orthodox Church. The Balkans have the Greek Orthodox Church. Egypt has the Coptic Church. Will it not be appropriate for all Western churches to quit India and let Indian Christians form their own Indian National Church?

□

Manu Maharaj Ki Jai!

Father surpasses a hundred teachers;
Mother surpasses a thousand fathers.

—*Manu Smriti*

The Rajasthan high court has planned to install a statue of Manu, the great law-giver. The statue is now ready; but there is opposition to its installation. There are some people who think Manu was anti-woman and anti-Harijan.

The ignorance of some people is impenetrable. Jesus and Mohammed accepted slavery, because it was normal in their age; are we, therefore, to think any the less of them?

It is true enough that Manu did not want the Shudras, being uneducated, to read the *Vedas*. But all ancient schools forbade such instruction to all and sundry, for fear of corruption and vulgarisation of the sacred texts. And in any case, was this ban very different from the current stipulation that those securing less than a certain percentage of marks, will not be admitted to college?

It is true enough that *Manu Smriti* in one place talks of red hot irons for their violating the above rule. But could this not be a medieval interpolation? For how could Manu, who asks people to speak the truth and speak it sweetly, or not at all (IV: 138), utter such crudity?

Again it is true that Manu prescribes different punishments for different castes *for* the same offence. But this again was universal ancient practice. We had the same thing in feudal Europe, until the Napoleonic Code took over. Also, while Shudras got more punishment for some offences, other castes got more punishment for some other offences. For example, for theft, the Vaishya had to pay double the fine of a Shudra, the Kshatriya, four times that, the Brahmin eight times or even hundred-fold. And a thieving king was to be fined a thousand fold! (VIII: 336-7-8).

Thanks to the Emergency of 1975-77, I could find the time to read Manu—and much else—in jail. I must say *Manu Smriti* is one of the greatest works of mankind. In all probability Manu was not an individual but whole generations of seers, who put together this distilled wisdom of the ages. Manu, *Manushya* and *Mann* (mind) all have the same Sanskrit-root, 'man' for man and mind.

Apart from the above reference, there is nothing in Manu to shock anybody. Obviously the portals of knowledge were open to bright Harijans. For Manu says: "A faithful man may receive pure knowledge even from a low-caste man; the highest virtue from the lowest, a jewel of a woman even from a bad family (II: 238). On the other hand he had no use for a Brahmin who was not learned. For him such a Brahmin was no better than an eunuch (II: 158). By marrying up—or down—"The Shudra attains Brahmanship and the Brahman attains Shudraship" (X: 65).

As for the women, Manu no doubt leaves them under the protection of father/husband/son. But, for the rest, he has the highest respect for motherhood. True, he permits beating of "wife, slave and pupil", but he also permits beating of son and younger brother (VIII: 299). However, it is significant that daughter and sister are not to be beaten. He goes on to say: "The daughter is equal to the son" (IX: 130).

It is not only modern society that says "women first". Manu said we must give the right of way to "the old, the sick, the man carrying a load, a woman, the king, the *snatak* just back from his Brahmacharya ashram, and the bridegroom" (II: 138).

He adds "A teacher surpasses in venerableness ten sub-teachers; a father, a hundred teachers, but a mother surpasses a thousand fathers" (II: 145). Again says Manu: "Where women are honoured, there gods rejoice, but where they are not honoured, there all rites are fruitless. Where women grieve, the family quickly

perishes; but where they do not grieve, that family ever prospers" (IV: 56-57).

In the face of all this, for anybody to say that Manu was anti-woman—or anti-Harijan—is to defame Manu and betray his own ignorance. Indeed Manu is so great, selections from the *Smriti* should be prescribed in school and college. Here are some gems:

"The lowest and highest incomes should be in the ratio 1:6" (VII: 26). Could any socialist go farther?

"Taxation should be as smooth—and painless—as the evaporation of water under the Sun" (IX: 305). Could a tax-harassed public wish for anything more?

"Anybody who hurts a tree must be punished" (VIII: 285). That would delight the environmentalists of the world.

"The first job of a conquering king should be to go and worship the gods of the conquered" (VII: 201). What could be a greater lesson in tolerance?

"Food should be given even to dogs, gently; and not roughly" (III: 92). Here is a gentleman to his fingertips.

That was Manu the Great. The only rational response to the ignorant denigration of Manu would be to name more and more children as 'Manu'!

□

Manu the Greatest

The Ordinances of Manu is a Work which is superior, and superior beyond comparison, which even to name in one breath with the Bible would be a sin against the Holy Ghost.

—*Nietsche*

Rath Yatra...Tazia....Ganeshotsav

Timurlang converted the Rath Yatra into the Tazia.

Sister Nivedita, the distinguished Western disciple of Swami Vivekanand, once said that if only the Hindus jointly prayed together just once a week—like Muslims and Christians—they would become a formidable force in the world. We Hindus haven't done that; by and large, when we do pray, we tend to do so alone, in the privacy of the home. But we have done the next best thing; we have evolved prolonged public celebrations of a religious nature. In Bengal and Eastern India, it is Durga Puja; in Western India it is Ganesh Utsav; and the two are tending to spread far and wide. Ganesh literally means Gan-esh (People's God). No wonder, therefore, that he is very popular with the masses.

There he sits, the elephant-god Ganesh, the 'Lord and Master of obstacles' with a mouse for his mount. And why not? As Heinrich Zimmer explains in his *Myths and Symbols in Indian Art and Civilization* (Harper & Row, New York, 1962): "Ganesh forges ahead through obstacles as an elephant through the jungle, but the mouse too is an overcomer of obstacles, and, as such, an appropriate, even though physically incongruous, mount for the gigantic pot-bellied divinity of the elephant head. The elephant passes through the wilderness, treading shrubs, bending and uprooting trees, fording rivers and lakes easily; the mouse can gain access to the bolted granary. The two represent the power of this god to vanquish every obstacle in the way."

Nor need the infinite variety of Divine forms—including the 'elephant god'—surprise the spiritually sophisticated. As Count Keyserling puts it in his memorable *Travel Diary of a Philosopher* (Harcourt Brace & Co., New York, 1925): "I have found the key to the problem of the Indian outlook on the world. The Indian regards psychic phenomena as fundamental; these phenomena are more real to him than physical ones... Hindu art alone has perhaps succeeded in manifesting invisible things in the visible world.... They were so conscious, on the one hand, of the inexpressibility of divinity, and, on the other, of the infinite number of possible manifestations, that generally they preferred the manifold expression to the simple one.... What is valuable—significance or facts? Significance alone; facts as such are totally irrelevant. Thus India with its tendency to producing myths, has, judged from the angle of life, chosen the better part of life as opposed to precise Europe....Most attention is paid to the idols, which are calculated to suit the poor man's power of understanding; thus, even in Banaras, the town of Shiva, Ganesh, the elephant-headed protector of earthly success, receives the richest sacrifices. The educated do not object to this; their philosophy approves and encourages every form of devotion. Their view teaches that all concepts of faith have the sole object of giving an aid to men to become conscious of their deepest selves."

Lord Sinha, the first Indian member of the Viceroy's Council, used to have a *murti* of Ganesh, the impish "remover of obstacles" in his Chambers. The unprecedented success of Lord Sinha in life made even his *Deva* popular in Bengal.

Today Ganesh is more popular in Maharashtra than any other deity. But until 250 years ago Ganesh was not all that much known in Western India. It was a Kannada nobleman in Pune who used to have Ganesh Puja at his residence, where he invited Pune *Sardars*. The year 1761 was a turning point in history; the Marathas lost the Third Battle of Panipat and the Nizam attacked and sacked Pune itself. It was only after these twin traumas that Ganesh as *Vighneshwar*, 'remover of obstacles', became really popular in Maharashtra.

However, until a hundred years back, Ganesh Puja—like all other Pujas—were a private affair. It was in 1893 that the great Lokmanya Bal Gangadhar Tilak for the first time made it a public affair. It was a stroke of genius that moved—and united—masses and classes alike. Overnight Tilak became Tilak Maharaj. It was like the recent Ram *Shilas* (consecrated Rama bricks) that electrified the whole country. It is significant that the first public Ganesh Puja came in the same year—1893—as Swami Vivekanand's historic address at the Chicago Congress of Religions. The country was awake and on the march.

Until Tilak Maharaj made Ganeshotsav public, all Hindu celebrations were home-bound or, at the most, temple-bound. Even on great festivals like Diwali, Dussehra, Holi, Makar Sankranti and Krishna Janmastami, there were no religious processions with mass mobilisation. That distinction went to the Muslims who mourned the death of Hassan and Hussain—Prophet Mohammed's grand-sons—for ten days, culminating in mass breast-beating, and the taking out of *Tazias* or *Tabuts*, as models of their tombs. Over the centuries, Hindus and Muslims had worked out a peaceful co-existence. Muslims freely joined Ramlilas etc., and Hindus had a participatory role in Moharram.

A huge mass of Muslim mourners dressed in black, with caparisoned horses—representing the mounts of Hassan and Hussain—and glittering *Tazias* made quite a spectacle. Over large parts of the country, Hindus, both men and women, collected in large numbers to see it. Some of them donated money and offered *sharbat* to the mourners. There was even a belief with some people that if a childless woman passed under a *Tazia*, she will become a mother before long.

As a child, I remember my father taking me on his shoulders to see the horse 'Dul Dul' dance. As young boys, we used to take vantage positions along the route to see the impressive Moharram procession. The occasion was sad; but a spectacle was a spectacle! The following day we would compare notes and each boy thought that his area *Tazia* was the best!

In Maharashtra, Hindus, made up as lions, used to dance in

front of *Tazias* as 'Moharram ke Sher'. However, all this camaraderie was disrupted by a number of developments. The Wahabi movement and the Tabligh Jamaat made Muslims fundamentalist and fanatical. For them, all Indian customs and practices were non-Muslim, and, therefore, un-Islamic and even anti-Islamic. They began to drift away from their Hindu brethren. The British fanned all these flames of separatism. In this situation, the Hindu became extra conscious of his heritage; if the Muslims kept away from Ramlila, why should the Hindus associate with Ids or Moharram?

This was the context in which Tilak made Ganeshotsav a public celebration. As he explained in his papers *Kesari* and *Mahratta*; "In the last 200-300 years, till a couple of years ago, some Hindus worshipped Muslim gods on Moharram. Our philosophy till now was that God is one But now, inspite of the fact that Hindus integrate with Muslims every year, if under the influence of some mischievous elements, they have forgotten the brotherhood of all these years, they have started fighting, troubling our devotees, even stooping to kill; if they do not have a change of heart or attitude then, though we have worshipped their *Pir*, it's time to ask if Hindus should dance in front of the *Tabut*." With the launching of Sarvajanik Ganeshotsav, Hindus stopped dancing in Moharram processions; they started singing and dancing in Ganesh procession; But even so, Ganesh charms some Muslims also. Some of them are regular visitors to Ganesh temples. And Najma Behn Heptullah has one of the finest collections of Ganesh icons.

Except for the fact that Moharram is mournful and Ganeshotsav is festive, there is a lot in common between the two. Both have a religious symbol—Ganesh or *Tabut*; both symbols are immersed in the waters; both involve the masses; both run for ten days, more actively at night than during day time. It is clear that Moharram provided a convenient model for Ganeshotsav. However, the interesting thing to note is that the *Tazia* or the *Tabut* itself is a purely Indian phenomenon both in its concept and its execution. It is unknown in the Arab world.

Islam does *not* permit the construction of graves, much less of tombs. A Muslim is expected to be buried level with the ground. That is why, when the orthodox Wahabi Sauds came to power in Arabia, they demolished the tombs that had come up over the centuries. The *Tazia*, as a representation of the grave of Hassan and Hussain, is, thus, quite un-Islamic. How it became part of Indian Islam makes interesting reading.

According to Maulana Sibtul Hassan, a scholar of repute, the *Tazia* was born in India about six hundred years ago (*vide The Hindustan Times*, Sunday Magazine, Oct. 31, 1982).

The Mongol warrior Timurlang (known in the West as 'Tamerlane', a corruption of 'Timur-lang', that is 'Timur the Lame') used to keep a copy of the Koran, a lock of the hair of the Prophet and some earth from Karbala—where Hussain is buried—in a leather bag on a horseback alongside his own stallion. While in India in 1398, Timur saw the *Raths* and *Rath Yatra*. He decided that the *Rath* or chariot was a more appropriate and a more respectful manner of carrying those relics than the back of a horse. That marked the birth of the *Tazia*. The *Tazia*, thus, was the child of the *Rath*.

And the *Rath* and the *Rath Yatra*—grand sire of today's Ganeshotsav—have a hoary history of their own. The oldest recorded *Rath Yatra* belongs to Puri Jagannath. The Trinity of Jagannath, (Krishna, Balaram and Subhadra)—goes back to prehistory. The images, made of wood, go back to tree worship and the sanctity of the environment. It is a clear case of a synthesis of plains and tribal people and culture. Here many of the priests were non-Brahmin. Lord Jagannath was 'Odisa Rajya Raja Sri Jagannath', king of Orissa; mortal royalty was only *Odya Sewakar* (first servant) of the Lord. When Muslims invaded Orissa, and the king fled to the jungle with the holy trinity, the Nawab pressed him to return and assured him security, because the presence of Lord Jagannath in Puri alone gave legitimacy to a Government.

In 1751, Marathas seized Orissa from the Nawab of Bengal. The Bhonslas of Nagpur became the devoted patrons of Jagannath. When the British wanted to occupy Orissa—to join up Bengal and Madras—they tried to find out under what conditions Marathas

would be willing to cede Orissa to them. The Marathas made it clear that their first condition was to retain complete control over Puri. The British, who knew the sovereign importance of Puri Jagannath as the moral monarch of Orissa, could not agree to that. In 1803 they forcibly occupied Orissa, including Puri.

The car of Jagannath has found its echo in the English language as 'Juggernaut', something huge, moving irresistibly. And meanwhile it was reborn as *Tazia* in the Muslim society and today it also stands reborn in Ganeshotsav processions in all its glory. Such is the power of people's religion. It is *Sanatana*.

There is a great good reason for the persistence of the spectacular in religion. Life can be drab; it can be exacting; the routine of life can be soul-killing. That being so, man needs some colour, some music in life. "All work and no play makes Jack a dull boy." You can't be 'correct' all the time. Some mirth and jollity, some gay abandon, some clapping and swaying to and fro, can melt away tensions and be good for health, physical and mental. That is why the Romans said man needed 'Bread and Circus'. The Greeks found their outlet for fun in Olympiad Festival, from which have derived the Olympic Games of modern times. The Hindus for this reason invented the Holi long ago. We had something like Holi even in the days of Buddha 2,500 years ago. (*vide Dhammapada*, The story of Balanakhatta Festival). The West has its Halloween for a little fun and a little foolery. Even the Hippies are basically a protest against a routinised life.

So man must have some opportunity for an emotional outlet. Such an outlet can be 'secular' or 'religious'. There is one difference: a secular outlet can easily degenerate into vulgarity and obscenity: a religious outlet is more likely to remain within bounds of propriety. There are 'reformers' who think that too much time and money is expended on Ganeshotsav and Durga Puja etc. And that reminds me. An American executive had a Japanese guest. The American was in a hurry for the two of them to catch a particular train. The Japanese, who tend to be relaxed, asked him how much time that particular train will save them. "Five minutes", was the reply. "And", said our Japanese friend, "what will we do with those

five minutes." That quite deflated the American in a hurry.

What makes our reformers think that the time and money 'saved' from Ganeshotsav etc., will be more usefully spend? In any case what can be more educative, more elevating and more integrative than the song and dance and colour and gong of Ganeshotsav?

The great Tilak answered these small reformers a hundred years ago when he said: "There are complaints that children's time is wasted. I am surprised that so far nobody has charged that housewives do not cook properly because they are in a hurry to see the Ganapati in the evenings! If a cricket match is in progress, schools are closed; that is not wasting of time, but praying to Lord Ganesh is wasting time! The kind of rich *Sanskars* that our children imbibe during these ten days is far more important than the education they get through the year in the school."

Another set of 'reformers' regret the money spent on Ganeshotsav etc. I am sure they would like the country not to play Holi, Diwali and Dussehra also,—nor any Id or Christmas—just to save money. But save money for what? One man's expenditure is another man's income. Money is not wasted; it only circulates faster! And in the process we have all this song and dance, gymnastics and illumination. In any case no price is too high to pay for all this rich experience and sheer joy. The great Tilak had a reply for these money-men also. "There are accusations that too much money is spent on the festival. The Hindu nation is not one of slaves. If people cannot live 8-10 days in enthusiasm and live it up spending some money, then a nation of such people is as good as dead."

Unfortunately for these pseudo-reformers, the nation is alive, well and laughing:

Ganpati Baba Moriya,
Purcha Varshi Lokar Aa!

□

Jai Mata Di!

Ae Ma teri surat se alag
Bhagawan ki surat kya hogi.

Our secular friends are so unnerved by the unstoppable rise of the BJP that they just don't know what to do next. In their desperation they have launched the lie that BJP is anti-woman!

And that reminds me. During the freedom struggle Englishmen were heard arguing against the Congress thus: "The Muslims are not with you; the Princes are not with you; the Scheduled Castes Federation is not with you; so, who is with you? Almost nobody!" But fact was that Congress at the time was a powerful movement and it voiced the aspirations of most of the people.

Today the position of BJP is similar to that of the Congress before 1947. When, therefore, I hear the detractors of BJP today say: "Muslims are against you; SC and ST are not with you; the South and the East also are not with you; you are opposed to women's aspirations etc.", I feel vastly amused. These friends do not know that BJP wins a higher percentage of SC and ST seats than even general seats; that women vote even more than men for BJP; that today the BJP is growing fastest in the East and the South; and that even Muslims are beginning to understand and appreciate the BJP position.

In the case of women our critics combine two lies into one: they say that Hindu society has always ill-treated women and that BJP has very much inherited that tradition. Fact is that India has always given women a high place in society and BJP has certainly inherited that rich tradition.

We not only have goddesses like Durga and Kali, Lakshmi and Saraswati, we even have a divinity that is half male and half female—Ardhaṇarishwar. Some of the Vedic *Rishis* were women. From Gargi and Maitreyi to Sita and Draupadi, and Mira Bai and Rani Jhansi, we have had a long line of women warriors, scholars, statesmen and saints.

The ignorant often portray Manu as anti-woman etc., without reading him. But it is Manu who says "Where women are honoured, there the gods rejoice; but where they are not honoured, all rites are fruitless. (III; 56).

Amaury de Riencourt, French social historian writes in his *Sex and Power in History* (Delta, 1974): "Foreign observers, from the Greek Megasthenes several centuries before Christ to the Muslim scholar Al-Biruni some fifteen hundred years later, testify to the good treatment wives received at the hands of their husbands, to their often excellent education and their close contact with literature and the arts, especially during the Gupta era. The completely natural attitude of Indians towards sex, and the care with which experts on the subject (for example, Vatsyayana, presumed author of the *Kamasutra*) emphasized the husband's obligations toward his wife, prove conclusively that woman was not treated as a mere object for man's enjoyment but had as much right as he had to share in this enjoyment. She may have been debarred from knowledge of the Scriptures, but not from enjoying the pleasures of life.... The result is that sexual morality was higher in Indian civilization than in any other: prostitution, except for a few *Devadasis*, was rare; heterosexuality was the rule, and homosexuality as rare as prostitution. By spiritualising and sacralising sex, Hinduism removed all traces of that sense of sinfulness that was to plague Western culture....

"In other respects, the degradation of woman's social position in India was largely the result of the Islamic invasions.... The contrast between the fate of woman in Muslim-dominated northern India and in the South where there was no Muslim occupation was

striking. Compared with the Muslim Sultanates of the Deccan, the social status and influence of women in the Southern Hindu empire of Vijayanagar was considerable. Women were often historians, accountants, judges, baliffs, and even guards in the palace—which would have been unthinkable under Muslim rule. Indeed, with Islam came *purdah* and many restrictions that had been unknown in pre-Islamic days, and often, for the sake of the protection of the women themselves, Hindu society embraced these restrictions wholeheartedly."

It is the stability of the Indian family that has given stability to our civilization and enabled us to survive the vicissitudes of history. No wonder when Mahmud Ghazni invaded India, his historian, Al-Biruni noted: "In all consultations and emergencies the Hindus take the advice of women." But under Muslim rule the position of women declined.

Since some Muslim males married several wives, many males had to go without a wife. This gave an impetus to prostitution—and to homosexuality. Child marriage and *Sati* also got impetus after the Islamic invasions. Since kidnapping of a woman was always a possibility, but normally married women were not kidnapped, girls—and boys—came to be married very young. Also the practice of *Sati* spread because a widow could be kidnapped or seduced. Even so, this evil practice was confined to the rich and the aristocratic, who were not too many. But the great Persian Sufi poet Hafiz even saluted the *Satis* thus; "Nobody is as brave in love as a Hindu wife; not many moths will burn themselves on an extinguished flame."

During all this period, the position of woman in other civilizations was not too good. Islam put them in *burqa* and the *zenana*, subject to polygamy and instant *talaq*.

Greece is the mother of Western civilization. It was a great civilization. But the position of women was none too good in ancient Greece. On one occasion a debate ensued among some Greek philosophers as to how many teeth women had. Since they considered women inferior, they decided that women had four teeth less than men; none of them suggested counting the teeth in a woman's mouth!

Women played a great role in the spread of Buddhism in China. They were attracted to Buddhist piety and pilgrimages. But the Chinese woman soon found her feet bound tight in infancy, so that she hobbled all her life.

Women also had a great role in the spread of Christianity in the West. In Mariolatry, the adoration of Mary, mother of Jesus, they found much solace and satisfaction. But that did not improve their position much; when crusaders left for Jerusalem in the Middle Ages, some of them left their womenfolk in chains—so that they did not go out and go astray.

During the Middle Ages they in the West burnt 'witches' by the thousand. The last case of "witch-burning" took place in USA in Boston as late as 19th century. Writes A. Sinclair in his *The Emancipation of the American Woman*: "American women were almost treated like Negro slaves, inside and outside the home. Both were expected to behave with deference and obedience towards owner or husband; both did not exist officially under the law; both had few rights and little education; both found it difficult to run away; both worked for their masters without pay; both had to breed on command, and to nurse the results."

Indeed the liberation of American womanhood came only with the emancipation of Negro slaves. Both in America and in England, feminist movement was an outcrop of the anti-slavery struggle. As Wallace, one of the early feminists and abolitionists put it in Sinclair's *The Emancipation of the American Woman*: "We have good cause to be grateful to the slave for the benefit we have received to *ourselves*, in working for *him*. In striving to strike his irons off, we found most surely, that *we* were manacled ourselves." Actually the American woman got the vote only after the American negro male. And the Englishwoman got her vote only in 1928. The American Declaration of Rights saying "All men are equal", in fact for long meant only that "All White Anglo-Saxon Protestant (WASP) Males are equal." However, none of these societies has ever gone about condemning themselves for not treating their womenfolk too well. We are the only ones engaged in self-

flagellation all the time.

Today the Western woman is very advanced. She has education, she has money, she has career. But she does not have a secure marriage or a happy old age. A young and handsome woman is a goddess; but an ageing woman, in the words of Picasso, is a doormat. There are too many one-parent families, with men abandoning their wives and children. The end-result is a gross neglect of the children who will constitute the next generation. On the other hand, as Swami Vivekanand observed: "the Indian woman has all the rights that really matter—life-long security, affection, respect." It is only in India that even a grown up man goes and touches his mother's feet. Only an Indian film could compose the song:

Ae Ma Teri Surat Se Alag
Bhagawan Ki Surat Kya Hogi.

(Oh mother, God sure does not look any different than you).

This is the great tradition of the power and sanctity of womanhood—*Matri Shakti*—that India has inherited through the ages and that the Sangha Parivar seeks to uphold. Not that there are no aberrations. And in any case, in a poor, subjugated country, everybody suffers, whether it is man or woman, young or old, 'upper' caste or 'lower' caste. But we have to understand the inwardness of this situation and not keep picking holes in Hindu society all the time.

When the British engaged an American lady, Catherine Mayo, to write *Mother India* alleging Hindu male ill-treatment of Hindu women, Gandhiji aptly described her as "inspectress of gutters". Every society has its gutters. But we don't have to be smelling gutters all the time. Let us look up to the Polar Star, *Dhruv Tara*, that is the model of fidelity in an Indian marriage and shout with joy, *JAI MATA DI!* (Glory unto the Mother!)

□

VIII. LAST BUT NOT THE LEAST

1. Population is Power!
2. Sex Symbols in Religion
3. The Greatness of Tipu Sultan
4. Ghalib: The Prophet of Hindu-Muslim Unity
5. The 'Good' British and the 'Bad' Muslim
6. Clash of Interests, not Civilizations
7. Politicians and the Stars

Population is Power!

The fear that haunts the West
is India and China.

—*Katherine & AFK Organski*

In the year 2000 the billionth Indian was born. Neither the government nor the people seem to be sure whether to congratulate ourselves or criticise ourselves on this occasion. And so government has done the best it can do in this situation. It has appointed a 100-member National Commission on Population to stabilise the population by the year 2045 by rewarding late marriages and the birth of girls.

This committee has any number of politicians, officials, doctors, actors and perhaps only poets and philosophers have been left out. They are all agreed that India's population must be 'controlled'. But you cannot switch off, or switch on, population.

Too many people take a simplistic, arithmetical view of life. They assume that if numbers go down, living standards would automatically and correspondingly go up. Not necessarily. In the US, both population and prosperity, have been going up. In Russia, both have been going down.

Also it is not realised that population is rising so dramatically in India not only because of the high birth-rate but because of the falling death-rate. And there are clear limits to the latter. Also it is forgotten that population is not just a problem, it is also a solution. As producers and consumers of goods and services, population is also power.

The West is not urging birth control to India for our good, but for their own advantage. As Organski, author of *Population and World Power* notes: "One of the fears that haunts the West today is that such crowded lands as China and India may continue to grow until they reach a point of such unbearable tension that they will send their people swarming across their borders into relatively empty lands, nearby."

It is significant that no western power has any policy to curb population; and many of them have policies encouraging births. Britain had a population of just five million at the time of battle of Plassey. Today, it has 50 million—plus many more millions gone to the US, Australia and elsewhere. In France, other things being equal, a family with three kids gets twice as much money as a family with no child. (Marshal Petain had attributed the collapse of France in World War II to 'too few children').

In Germany, the government wants to have Indian computer engineers. However the cry has gone up that "We want (more) children and not Indians" (*Kinder Statt Inder*).

In Russia, there is a four-month maternity leave. (Some Scandinavian countries have even introduced paternity leave). Italy and Spain are worried about their stagnant population. A major factor in America's growth is an unending 'baby boom'. Although family planning has been widely practised in Japan since World War II, the country is not happy with its consequences. Former Japanese premier Sato, who visited India in 1971, advised us against it.

Some people talk of China's 'one-child plan'. But the ground reality is very different. In 1957, Mao Zedong had proposed a stable population of 600 million. But today it is already 1,100 million. Beijing's *Renkon Yanjin* (29.3.1999) reported: "There is no unified family planning law in the country. Marriages between persons belonging to different regions and communities have taken place and there is no law governing the birth of children in such marriages. There are also problems of refusal to abide by the law. Family planning cadres ask, and receive, bribes. It is hard to manage the growing floating population. People move places to evade the family planning law. The place of emigration can do nothing, while the place of immigration does not want to do anything."

On the map, China looks much bigger than India. But fact is that India has more cultivable land—and more water—per head than China. The point to ponder is: If China with less land can maintain a bigger population at a higher standard of living, why can't we?

This being the situation in all the major countries of the world, we need to give more serious thought to the subject. For example some countries—and societies—are growing much faster than others. This can only lead to massive population movements across national frontiers, resulting in confrontations and even conflicts. What the world, therefore, needs is a global population policy. Globalisation without a uniform global population policy could have very serious consequences.

While this is not going to materialise any time soon, India must work for a uniform population policy at least in South Asia. Today the fact is that Pakistan and Bangladesh have populations which are growing faster than India's. That is why 20 million Bangladeshis have already crossed over to India. And if, as and when India-Pakistan relations improve, we can expect a similar flood from Pakistan. New Delhi must, therefore, hasten slowly with population stabilisation, until such time as our neighbours agree to follow a similar policy.

The Indian public is not unaware of the inwardness of the world population situation. No wonder when the government called an all-party MPs meeting some time back—on the issue of barring those with more than two children from contesting elections—only the CPI and Shiv Sena backed the proposal. All other party representatives categorically rejected it.

In this situation, we don't have to push through a policy framework that no other major country is inclined to adopt. We don't have to go in for pills and loops and vasectomies and tubectomies. They all have serious physical and psychological side-effects. We can leave it all to education and awareness. We can also encourage mothers to prolong breast-feeding, which is known to delay the next pregnancy. (On the other hand, abortions are often followed by quick second pregnancies.)

We need to remind ourselves of what Colin Clark, economist and philosopher, has had to say about India: "Population pressure is probably the only force strong enough to overcome the intense conservatism of the Indian peasant. In the unlikely event of family limitation, most of the stimulus to economic development would be removed with it." He added that he knew of several civilizations—including Greek and Roman—that collapsed due to under-population, but he did not know any that died of over-population.

□

Population & World Power

A population of great size inspires confidence at home and fear and respect abroad.

The four great giants–China, India, Russia and the United States–will retain a position that lesser nations cannot rival. Unification of small neighbours into new nations could conceivably produce new giants....

"India is potentially a nation of greater power than either the United States or Russia....The second place in world power should be hers....

"China....is starting where Russia left off. It is quite possible that India, starting still later than China, will devise an even more effective system and surpass China in modernity and in living standards...."

–Katherine Organski & AFR Organski:
'Population & World Power'

Sex Symbols in Religion

It is madness, almost a crime against the Holy Ghost, to ban eroticism from life.

—Count Hermann Keyserling

A few years back the Supreme Court held that Anand Margis could not be told to refrain from dancing with a skull in one hand and a dagger in the other, since that is their religious faith and practice. I have never understood Anand Margis, but that is probably my own limitation. However, I am glad the Supreme Court has upheld their religious right—so long as they do no harm to anybody else. Assuming the Anand Margis are 'wrong', does not democracy give man 'the right to be wrong'? After all who is to decide what is right and wrong? I hope the government does not try to override the Supreme Court judgement by a constitutional amendment. For governments have the tendency to act as if they were omniscient gods.

A couple of years earlier the Karnataka government banned an ancient local custom of devotees appearing naked before their deity once in a year. More recently that state government came down with a heavy hand on Belgaum's ancient Yellamma temple practice of initiating *devadasis* and *jogappas*. And the other day the Kerala government came out against the ancient practice of *Kavuthendal* in the Bhagwati temple at Kodungallur. This practice allows 'untouchables' to 'pollute' the temple with ribald songs, since the goddess Kannaki, neglected by her libertine spouse, is believed to enjoy the same!

All these practices may make no sense to English-educated urbanites like you and me. But they obviously mean much to their rural practitioners, and we have no right to impose our style or taste on them as long as they don't do any violence to anybody else. In the case of the Karnataka *pujas* in the nude, I wish the government had banned cameras—which were an intrusion into the temple—and not the devotees, who were only minding their customary religious business as they understand it. Custom overrides the law. As Dostoevsky made Dimitry say in his classic *Brothers Karamazov*: "What seems disgraceful and dishonouring to the intelligence appears as pure beauty to the heart. So does beauty lie in Sodom? Believe me she lives in Sodom for the majority of men... it is awful that beauty is not only terrible but also mysterious. There the Devil wrestles with God—and the battlefield is the human heart."

Nor need any prurient puritan think lightly of sex symbols in religious worship. The roots of religion lie in joy and wonder, and sex exemplifies both. As Count Keyserling, author of the famous *Travel Diary of a Philosopher* noted after a visit to Madurai in the last century: "Here, for the first time in my life, I behold the display of sexual activity, not regarded as something unclean, but as something holy, as symbolising the divine in nature. There was no obscene association in the minds of the faithful present at the feast of Rameshvaram, who beheld the union of Shiva and Shakti symbolised by puppets. None of the women who bowed before the *lingam* tonight seemed to differ in their attitude from that of a Spanish nun who prays to the ideal of the Immaculate Conception. Every Hindu devotee reveres sensual love as the image of divine creative force and uses it as the vehicle of pious thoughts of sacrifice. The *Shastras* teach that man and wife shall never approach each other without thinking that, in this way, Brahma is acting through them. They are taught to honour each other as divine while they love one another, not in the spirit of carnal enjoyment, but in the sense of a god-like pouring-out of life. Thus animal instincts are sanctified as the expression of divinity." He added: "It is madness, almost a crime against the Holy Ghost, to ban

eroticism from life, as the puritanism of all countries and all times had done: it signifies, in reality, the fulcrum of human nature. Through the eros every string of his being can be set in motion, and the deepest reverberations have generally emanated from it." Even the Cross, Dome and the Minaret are believed to be sexual symbols.

India has always taken a relaxed view of sex. Here sex is not sin, but sacrament. And so you have the temple of Khajuraho where sex is literally celebrated. This was so in the West also, until the Church came up with its West Asian puritanical ideas. Right now Michelangelo's immortal paintings are being cleared and cleaned of soot and dust in the Vatican. And they find that in their puritanism the Church authorities had painted over some of the masterpieces to hide the angels' anatomy! Of course such denial of life takes its own revenge. There are Church panels in Italy showing erection of holy fathers through their vestments!

Here a clear distinction needs to be made between religious and commercial expressions of sex. Where a practice is old and customary, it may not be interfered with. Where, however, the object is to vulgarise and titillate with a view to making money, it may be curbed. That, in brief, is the difference between art and obscenity.

Certain practices may appear rude and vulgar, and not to our taste. But we don't have to fit everybody to our taste. Let time and circumstances change tastes gradually, as is the way of nature. Scientists and social philosophers think that the human species may die of impotence or boredom. Anything, therefore, that lends colour to life and makes it less boring, should be welcome as a factor for life. Perhaps playing Holi—and even a little levity, now and then—is not such a bad thing after all, as any psychiatrist will tell you. Nor need anybody be shocked by the traditional Naga *sadhu* processions at Kumbh Melas. The man designated Shankaracharya of Puri has to bathe naked in the sea before he can be anointed. Mature men—and women—don't have to be prudishly shocked by these ancient practices; they should try to understand them—and understand the genesis of religion. □

The Greatness of Tipu Sultan

He was in touch with American & French Revolutionaries!

A few years back, Doordarshan telecast the serial on Tipu Sultan. Some friends, particularly in Kerala, had strong objection to any serial on Tipu. Their argument was that he had invaded Malabar, despoiled the land, desecrated temples and forcibly converted many Hindus.

Accounts differ as to the dimensions and motivation of that sorry enterprise. While some people attribute it to the communalism of Tipu, others explain it as part of Tipu's war with the British and with the trading allies of the British on the west coast.

In this connection the letters of Tipu's sons have been produced to indict Tipu. Here the position is that the British had increased the allowances of Tipu's sons by 600 per cent. (The Maharana of Udaipur used to draw Rs 1000 a month: when he came under the wings of the British they told him he could draw Rs 1000 a day!) This was the British way of binding princes to their rule with chains of gold.

Matters have been further confused by British forgeries and propaganda, candidly described by Lord Curzon as 'the furniture of empire'. But there is no doubt that the 18th century in India was the age of *Thugs* and *Pindaris*. It was a time when, in the words of Clive, "Sovereignty had fallen to the ground for anybody to pick it up." Excesses, therefore, were no doubt committed

in Malabar and other places. Although these excesses were committed by Tipu's underlings, the constructive responsibility was obviously that of Tipu himself. So the Malabar episode is certainly a black mark against Tipu.

But here it is important to note that history is the story of heroes; and heroes are rarely saints. If we were to take note of negative factors in heroic lives it would not be possible to okay any historical serial. I will give just two examples.

Ashoka invaded Kalinga and, in the battles that ensued, one lakh people were killed. Would any TV serial on Ashoka show that tragedy? Or would Ashoka be disqualified from a TV serial?

Banda Bairagi was a great hero; but in his anger against Muslim excesses, he had killed some 30,000 Muslims in the city of Sirhind, Punjab. Would this incident be reason enough not to have a serial on Banda Bairagi? I suppose a time comes when we have to push to the back of the mind those "old, unhappy far-off things and battles long ago".

Every nation needs heroes—and villains. They define a nation's hopes and fears. We in India, apart from ancient and modern heroes, have many in the middle ages—Shivaji, Rana Pratap, Guru Govind Singh, Krishnadeva Raya, Rani of Jhansi. We also have villains in Mohammed Bin Qasim, Mahmud Ghazni, Mohammed Ghori, Allauddin, Aurangzeb, Nadir Shah, Ahmed Shah Abdali. I submit that men like Akbar, Dara Shikoh and Tipu Sultan qualify as heroes and not as villains.

Indeed, the more I read about Tipu the more I am impressed with his rich personality. Young Tipu had two tutors: one Hindu—Pandit Govardhan—and one Muslim—Maulvi Obaidullah. His life-long companion and Prime Minister was Purnaiyya; his commander-in-chief was Krishna Rao; his private secretary was one Shivaji. He had endowed 156 temples. Every morning the first thing he did was to take his bath and bow to the deity, Sri Ranga. On one occasion when he did not get up to greet Shringeri Maharaj, he apologised for his lapse and performed *shat-chandi-yagna*, by way of *prayaschit*. And, of course, he was the only prince who died fighting the British. The symbol on his flag was a tiger, and to this day the British Museum has Tipu's mechanical tiger with a British soldier in its claws; when this tiger roars, the Englishman under him trembles in terror.

Tipu did not content himself with fighting the British; he tried to give his territories—covering parts of all the four southern states—a really advanced administration. He forbade forced labour for public works and torture of suspects; he introduced prohibition; he forbade felling of trees or hunting of animals; he tried to set up a school every four miles. When he found that effluents from an ammunition factory were polluting the river Kaveri, he had the factory shifted. Here was a model ruler for environmentalists.

The ruler gave Mysore its silk, sandalwood and pearl industries. He reformed weights and measures and corrected even the Hijri calendar. And like a multinational corporation of today, he set up trading posts in Kutch, Hormuz, Jeddah, Aden and Basra!

Even while doing all this, Tipu found time to read books! On the occasion of his marriage, his father Hyder Ali asked him what he would like to have for a wedding gift. And do you know what Tipu's choice was? A library! Hyder Ali had many books collected in India and abroad and had the English and French books translated for him in Persian. (The first thing the 'enlightened' British did after the fall of Tipu was to burn this library!)

Perhaps what surprises me most about Tipu is his wide outlook. A fatal flaw with most medieval Indian princes was that they could not look beyond their principalities; they had no conception of India. Indeed, that was why first the Turks, and then the British, were able to overwhelm India. While the Indian princes could not look beyond their dynastic noses, the invaders saw India as one and whole; unless they controlled the whole country they could not be sure of holding any part of it. That is why Allauddin Khilji drove down to Madurai, and that is again why the British drove up to the Khyber Pass and beyond. Almost alone among Indian princes, Tipu had a world-view.

He had put up clocks from different countries showing the time in those countries. He sent embassies to Iran, Turkey and Mauritius, and a delegation to France. He was in correspondence with

Napoleon. He was thrilled to read the American Declaration of Independence. He sent Benjamin Franklin a donation as his contribution to the American war effort. And he greeted American Independence with a 108-gun salute! That was Tipu Sultan.

It has been said that Tipu was taking French help to fight the British, and that was not very patriotic. But then there was not a single Indian prince fighting the British, who did not take French advice in military tactics and weapons training. Ranjit Singh did the same. They were hiring Frenchmen to help fight the British; they were not playing second fiddle to the French.

Here was Tipu giving the British the fight of their life. Warren Hastings, the first British governor-general, found the Treaty of Mangalore with Tipu 'humiliating'. Tipu threatened to capture Madras, actually drew a cartoon in which the governor and his council were shown on their knees before Tipu, who held the governor's nose, elongated into an elephant's trunk, which poured forth gold and diamonds as tribute to Tipu, while the English commander-in-chief was shown holding the treaty in his hand, and breaking his sword in two, as symbolic of surrender!

Years later, thanks to overwhelming British force, aided by the treacherous Nizam, when Tipu fell in 1799, Wellesley, the governor-general raised his glass and said: "Ladies and gentlemen, I drink to the corpse of India." He was right; with the death of Tipu Indian independence had been extinguished for a century-and-a-half.

If he so desired, Tipu could have certainly bowed to the British and survived as a prince—as another His Exalted Highness. And today his great-great-grandsons would not be pushing cycle-rickshaws in the streets of Calcutta. But Tipu preferred death to dishonour. Alone among the princes of the 18th century, he died fighting the foreigner. Independent India cannot but salute Tiger Tipu.

□

Ghalib: The Prophet of Hindu-Muslim Unity

The World has not gone to pieces only because of Kashi Vishwanath!

—*Ghalib*

Doordarshan deserves to be congratulated for *Mirza Ghalib*. Its earlier forays into history, *Bahadur Shah Zafar* and *Amir Khusro*, were almost sub-standard. *Bahadur Shah* was not only unhistorical in many parts, it sounded more like 'Ashok Bahadur'. And *Amir Khusro* was a tiresome sermon on 'secularism'. In comparison, *Mirza Ghalib* is excellent. Not only is there no attempt at any propaganda, Naseeruddin Shah does full justice to the character he portrays.

The only problem with this serial is that its Urdu will not be easily understood east of the Ganga or south of the Narmada. But then this was an insoluble problem; if it had been 'Hindised', Ghalib would have lost much of its original flavour. It is interesting to note that Ghalib wrote a lot in Persian, and his Persian poetry is better than his efforts in Urdu. But today, nobody reads his Persian verses, either in India or in Iran.

Ghalib is the best-known Urdu poet. And yet his poetry is not great. Poetry can't be great unless it has a moral dimension. And all Urdu poetry is 'secular'—it is mostly about wine and woman. If, therefore, you want to read great Indian poetry, you have to turn to spiritualists like Tulsi and Mira, Sur and Kabir,

Jaidev and Dnyaneshwar, Chaitanya and Chandidas, Alvars and Nayanars. But you do *not* want to read great poetry all the time for elevation; you also like to be amused and entertained. And in that genre there is nothing like Urdu poetry. It's lyrical, lilting and very lively. Just listen to Ghalib:

Ishq ne Ghalib nikamma kar diya
Varna hum bhi admi they kaam ke.

(Love has emasculated me; otherwise I too would have done something worthwhile.)

When Jawaharlal read it, the romantic in him promptly put it on its head to read:

Kaam ne Ghalib nikamma kar diya
Varna hum bhi admi they ishq ke.

(Grinding work has finished me; otherwise I too would have been a man of love.)

Ghalib's misfortune was that he was born at a time (Agra, 1797) when the Mughal Empire was dying. Actually it died (1857) before his death (1869). This twilight was a nightmare of want for Ghalib. But through penury and tribulations, Ghalib laughs and produces poetry that is moving because it is so tragic, so human. He was forever in need, not only because his pension was always shrinking, but because he had a great weakness for wine and women. His average for a good night was six bottles of gin ('Old Tom') and on one occasion it was as many as sixteen! And with every sip he took four almonds fried in *ghee*!

"They have indeed told you that wine is forbidden.
It's just a lie, told with good intent.
The very air is intoxicated;
He who breathes, also drinks."

He was fond of women, particularly of the dancing, 'low class' *Domin*. He actually borrowed money to buy jewellery for this lady.

"We will dismiss the *Saki*,
Turn out our friends and music-makers,
And kiss each other with an abandon.
That will make the stars quiver and blush."

Many a time he had no money even for food. ("I spent the Ramzan, eating fasts.") At other times, his house leaked like a sieve, and he had no quilt to cover himself during the winter. He writes to his friend Har Gopal 'Tufta': "Both you and I are fairly good poets. Agreed that some day we might become renowned like Saadi and Hafiz. But what did *they* gain, that we would?" And so he converted his house into a gambling den—and was hauled off to jail in chains!

Innumerable tomes have been written about 1857. But Ghalib's sidelights on the tumultuous events bring the trauma to life more effectively than anything else. He himself survived only because he was living in Ballimaran near the *haveli* of Hakims, medical consultants to the Maharaja of Patiala who was an ally of the British in 1857. As soon as the fighting was over, looting began: "Each soldier of England is now a potentate. Men are mortally scared to go out in the *bazaar*. The *Chowk* is the execution ground, the homes, dungeons. Each speaks of Delhi's dust, is thirsty for Muslim blood." And again: "The moon-faced *Begums* of the Red Fort are wandering around in the street in filthy clothes, ragged pyjamas and broken shoes....I, who cannot bear to see others begging from door to door, must myself beg."

In Delhi, among the Muslim nobility, "only three survive. Mustafa Khan in Delhi, Maulvi Sadruddin in Sultanji (Nizamuddin) and in Ballimaran this dog of the world called Asad." He tells his correspondent not to use his old Mughal titles while addressing him in letters because even that might get him into trouble! The British now decided to impose Octroi or 'Town Duty'. The people heard it as 'Pon Tooti'. And so Ghalib wrote: "Something like *Pon Tooti* has been levied on everything except grains and dung-cakes."

He notes that Muslims in general have been told to leave Delhi; their houses have been confiscated. As late as December 5, 1857 he wrote: "I cannot stir out of the house. Who is there in town to visit? The homes are deserted and lampless. Martial law is in force since May 11. Let's wait and see if the Muslims are allowed to resume living in Delhi." Later he reported with some hope: "According to a rumour, 5000 tickets have been printed; any Muslim who wants to live in Delhi must give a *nazarana* to the British officials and get the ticket to live within the city walls."

All of Ghalib's poems were lost to him. "I have not given up writing. Writing has given me up." And then he hears a beggar recite his poetry. Verily, out of death comes life. Writes Ghalib: "There is plenty of 'French' and 'Champagne' in the Parsi shops here. The *sahukars* are rolling in wealth and jewels. What difference does it make to me?"

Ghalib had always been an Anglophile. And now he composed 'Dastambu' (bouquet) in Persian in praise of the British role in 1857. When, long before 1857, Sir Syed Ahmed Khan asked him to do a commentary on Abul Fazal's *Ain-e-Akbari*, he had rejected the whole idea as ridiculous and wrote back: "Look at the *sahibs* of England. They have gone far ahead of our forbears. Wind and wave they have rendered useless. They are sailing their ships under fire and steam. With their magic, words fly through the air like birds. Air has been set on fire. Cities are being lighted without oil-lamps. This new law makes all other laws obsolete. Why must you pick up straws out of old, time-swept barns, while a treasure-trove of pearls lies at your feet?"

However, Ghalib never lost his pride. Even in his abject poverty he maintained many servants. Once he applied for a job in what is now Zakir Hussain College (the erstwhile Delhi College) outside Ajmeri Gate, Delhi. He arrived for the interview in his *palki* but since nobody from the college came out to welcome him, he left in disgust. He would not like to serve Englishmen who were so lacking in good manners!

What is the philosophy of Ghalib? It is: "Eat, drink and be merry."

"Eye-like under the eye-brow,
The tavern should be close by the arched mosque
Though from the Zoroastrian they received wine as his *Jaziya*
To me they served it in Ramzan, on a Friday even."

He finds paradise much too boring.

"To live with one single *hoori* till all eternity is an alarming thought indeed." And so he prays to God:

"Do add hell to the Elysian Fields, O Lord!
Let's have more fun in the after-life."

And, of course, Ghalib is a man of wide sympathies. "I consider all humanity to be my family. Every man, be he Muslim, Hindu or Christian, is my brother. Others may not accept it, but it does not matter."

Ghalib comes perilously close to apostasy ('Kufr') when he writes:

"Torn between true faith and the heretic view
I am pursued by the old, beckoned by the new."

In his Persian poem *Chiragh-i-Dair* (Temple Lamps) he asks a heavenly being why, when the world had gone to the dogs, the end had not come yet. And the heavenly spirit says:

Sua Kashi be andaze isharat,
Tabassum kardo gufta Een Imarat!

(Pointing to Kashi, he smiled and said that the world had not gone to pieces only because of that.) One wishes this great poem were rendered in Urdu and Hindi. That was Ghalib—tragic, lively, inimitable. Ghalib can unite Hindu and Muslim hearts more than any number of laws or sermons. He was only too right when he said: "Monumental that we are, Forget us not; For we are legends." □

Love has made me an infidel

Ruh ba aql ast o ilm ast yar,
Ruh ra ba Hindu o Muslim Chikar?

—*Rumi*

(The soul is concerned with wisdom and knowledge; what does it have to do with Hindu or Muslim?)

★

Mussalman gar bi-daniste ke Butt Cheest
Be daniste ke dindar But-Parast ast

—*Shabitsari*

(If the Muslim but knew the idol's meaning, in image worship would he see True Faith.)

The 'Good' British and the 'Bad' Muslim

The Muslim rule is over but the Hindu rule has not yet come....

—Bankim Chandra Chatterji

Mahatma Gandhi used to say that the British had exploited and hurt India more than the Muslim rulers. He was very right. But popular perception is different.

Muslim rule basically was Turkish rule. Though the Turkish rulers were foreigners, after a generation or two, they became quite Indianised. With the British, it was the other way round. To begin with, they appeared Indianised but became distant as soon as they established themselves. Yet Hindu perception of British rule is not a fraction as negative as that of Turkish rule.

The Turkish period was full of wars. But most of the loot remained within the country. Within the country, there was massive forcible transfer of land and other wealth in favour of invading Muslims. But most of the trade remained in Hindu hands.

Under British rule the transfer of wealth was massive and irretrievable. It was this wealth that financed the Industrial Revolution of England. But after 1857, the British continued to exploit India covertly. Their industrial policy favoured British industry at the cost of Indian industry. But since this exploitation was not accompanied by violence, as in the case of Turkish exploitation, it did not generate the same bitter opposition.

At the close of Muslim rule, India was rich enough to attract rival Western powers. At the close of British rule, India had been sucked dry. Turkish rule continued in India for five centuries. British rule lasted less than 200 years. Both tried to give India political and economic unity. While the British contribution to this unity is recognised, the Turkish contribution is not.

There was, however, a qualitative difference between Turkish and British rule. And that was the use of force. The British used force only to tip the balance. The Turks used the sword as a balance. The British won India through diplomacy reinforced by military force. The Turk ruled by force and slaughtered large numbers, destroyed temples, often forcibly converted people and even kidnapped women. All this outraged people.

How do we account for the very different behaviour of these two sets of conquerors? The basic reasons are two: the two conquests came in different eras, and they came from two very different quarters.

For centuries, the Christians were as intolerant and violent as the Muslims. The Spaniards played havoc with American Indians. The Portuguese did not behave much better on our West coast. But much of Europe had been reformed and civilised by the Renaissance. Contact with India, China and Persia had convinced thoughtful men in the West like Voltaire that there were alternative religions and civilizations with equal claims to human acceptance. The post-renaissance British and French were too civilized to behave like the Turks who invaded India.

Another factor was the different cultural background of the Turks and West Europeans. The Turks came from the wilds of Central Asia, with little cultural background. Even Amir Khusro was shocked to see the wild Mongol hordes, with their "hair falling into their eyes and their nasal hair getting into their mouth." He said the skin of Mongols was fit only for making shoes. But the Europeans had the background of the Roman Law and Empire. Senior British administrators who ruled India had studied Greek and Latin, and imbibed the humanist values of those two civilizations. Even in their imperial hauteur, they tended to follow the law.

Although for many years they did not let Indian judges try Englishmen, they would not let guilty whites go scot-free. In 1851, before the British occupied Lahore, some drunken English soldiers killed Col. Jiwan Singh in Amritsar. The British court sentenced the accused to death and Lord Dalhousie refused to commute their sentence. This perception of the British sense of fairplay played no mean part in Indian acceptance of British rule as the instrument for restoration of law and order.

Bankim Chandra Chatterjee clearly brings out the contrast between British and Muslim rules in his epochal *Anand Math*. The *Sanyasis* were up in arms against foreign rule. They had defeated the Muslim army and now they wanted to fight the British also but the head *Sanyasi* tells them: "No doubt, the Muslim rule is over and Hindu rule has not yet been established. But unless the British take over, there is no possibility of the revival of *Sanatan Dharma.* We shall advance towards the spiritual by mastering the secular through the medium of English education. Then there will be no hurdle in the way of spreading the *Sanatan Dharma.* The true *Dharma* will rise once again. Until that happens, until the Hindus become knowledgeable, accomplished and powerful, the British will continue to rule."

This is also the general Hindu view of British and Turkish rule though, in reality, it is difficult to tell which was worse. The British reinforced their partisan view of history through books and, in Curzon's words, other "furniture of empire", showing Muslim rule in bad light and British rule in good light. What India needs is a more balanced view of history.

□

Saffron is Sacred

In Arabia, the Koran is printed in Saffron.

The traditional wedding dress in Arabia is saffron.

The blessing in *Taawiz* (amulet) is written in saffron.

The royal Mughal seal was saffron.

Clash of Interests, not Civilizations

Huntington is wrong, he is only diverting attention.

A few years back Prof. Samuel Huntington of Harvard University came up with the high-sounding thesis that wars in future will not be fought between nations, but between civilizations. And he said there were eight civilizations: the Christian West, Muslim West Asia, Hindu India, Confucian China, Shinto Japan, Orthodox Christian Russia & the Balkans, Latin America and Africa. His fear was that China and the Muslim World may join hands to challenge the West. I have a shrewd suspicion that Huntington thought up the 'clash of civilizations' only to divert attention from the very real clash of interests.

There has always been a great variety of civilizations and cultures. When two major unfamiliar civilizations come face to face, there is some surprise, some curiosity, some comparisons, some contrasts, even some exchange of goods, services and ideas. But these civilizations do not clash unless vital interests are at stake, and there is a feeling that one side is trying to unfairly get the better of the other. When Alexander faced Porus, the latter told him they did not have to fight for gold or diamonds; whoever had more of it, could give some to the other. "But if you have come to take away my water, there will be war."

When Europeans first landed in the New World, they were almost welcomed. Trouble began only when the Whites started taking over Red Indian lands and other resources and bossing over them.

Ages ago some Arabs came to Malabar coast for trade; many Muslim tribes came from Central Asia and lived peacefully in and around Delhi. (Earlier the Prophet of Islam had said he got cool breezes from India.) Trouble began only when Mahmud Ghazni invaded India to loot its wealth—and did so in the booming name of Islam.

Relations between Western Europe and West Asia were soured by the Crusades. And the Crusades were ostensibly launched by the Church to retrieve the Cross on which Jesus was believed to have been crucified. Of course there was no Cross to retrieve; contemporary records show that Jesus was hanged from a tree and not crucified on the cross. The real reason for the eight Crusades—from 1095 to 1291—was that West Asia was much richer than Europe, and the latter wanted its fleshpots. The Pope admitted as much in his address to the Children's Crusade.

However, as civilizations, even during the Crusades, Muslim-Christian relations were sporty enough. Saladin, leader of the Muslim side, sent his doctor to see Richard the Lion-Hearted, leader of the Christian camp, when the latter fell ill!

Same is the story of European penetration of Africa. Sir Cecil Rhodes, who gave his name to Rhodesia—now Zimbabwe—was once asked if he had gone to Africa to spread civilization, and he said, no; he had gone there because he just could not any longer stand the rotten meat of England.

It will thus be seen that basically there was no difference between Mahmud Ghazni, Crusaders and the Conquistadors of the New World. They were all there for secular loot, in the name of Allah or the 'Son of God'. But at the civilizational level, different civilizations lived peacefully enough.

In India Hindu and Muslim kings fought for territory, wealth and power; the people didn't go about stabbing each other. Kabir said : "*Ram Rahim Ek Hai, Kashi-Kaaba Ek Hai*". Sant Tukaram said : "Before initiating anything, take the name of Allah." Urdu is seventy-five per cent Hindi; *Salwar* is very much a stitched up *dhoti*; Haj—complete with shaved head, unstiched white clothing, abstinence and *parikrama* of Qaaba sanctum—very much reminds

you of a Hindu pilgrimage. Aurangzeb imposed *Jaziya* in the name of Islam but the real reason was that his expansionist wars in the Deccan had emptied his treasury and he desperately needed money. For the rest, Mughal Government was a coalition of Turanis and Rajputs. And the Mughal Emperors celebrated not only Ids and Nauroz, the Persian New Year, but also Diwali and Dussehra, Holi and Basant. And they drank only *Ganga-jal*. Meanwhile regular trading *caravans* connected Banaras with Baghdad. Today India is politically divided. But we have not ceased to be One People. As Mao Tse-tung told Arshad Hussain, Pakistan Foreign Minister in Beijing in 1968 : "Tell me what is the difference between you and Indians? You look alike to me. Aren't you only temporarily separated from the Indians?"

India and the West are very different civilizations. But apart from beef, they have never quarrelled over civilizational issues. And even there, more and more Westerners have been going fully vegetarian. For the rest, the West loved our dance, our *Yoga*, our *Sari*, our herbs, our Gurus. Great Englishmen like Hastings and Curzon, great Frenchmen like Romain Rolland and Malraux, great Germans like Goethe and Max Muller and great Americans like Thoreau and Walt Whitman were great admirers of India. The real dispute during our Freedom Movement was over secular issues like the exchange rate of the rupee, the destruction of our textile industry and the share in political power and in the services, civil and military.

India and China have been very different but very friendly civilizations since ancient times. Apart from Mohammed Tughlaq who sent out an army to China—which army just evaporated in Tibet—we have had no problems until our inexplicable border dispute in recent years. Actually until the Middle Ages when Central Asian attacks pulverised India, China looked upon India as the Middle Kingdom (Chung-Kuo) or in modern terms, the "sole super power" of the times. Mao once told Nehru that traditional Chinese believed that good men were rewarded with birth in India in their next life.

China and the Muslim world are different civilizations but

they meet in Central Asia. The Muslim presence has been much less in China than in India. But even so, Ibn Batuta saw a *Kazi*, a Sheikh and a Sufi in every Chinese town. Marco Polo said the Chinese hated the Muslims. The Chinese were surprised by the Muslim rejection of pork and referred to them as 'pig mouth' (p'ing-tsui) and 'pig tail' (hiao chu-tan) etc. Only ten per cent of Chinese Muslims are Han by race; the other ninety per cent are Uighur in Sinkiang, known as 'Hui Hui' (Central Asian Russian word for penis, an obvious reference to their circumcision). Traditionally the Muslim in China was a horse trader and in that business he made good money and excited some envy. But the Chinese also noted appreciatively that there were no orphans and no prostitutes in Muslim Society.

In the Nineteenth century there was much Han-Hui violence in Kansu and Sinkiang. The Chinese going to Haj via India also brought back the germ of *Jehad*. But after the incorporation of those two provinces in China, Muslim separatism became a marginal issue.

Although the Crescent-Cross confrontation has been there for ages, fact is that both, Christianity and Islam are credal, semitic religions. While the traditional Hindu has many taboos vis-a-vis Christians, Muslims object only to pork, and Christians are familiar with that particular semitic taboo in their long-time association with Jews. The real problem is that the West has terminated Muslim influence in the world. On top of that West Asian Oil is filling Western coffers, but West Asian Oil earnings are going into the pointless purchase of arms and the obscene opulence of princes backed by the West. As the Muslims see it, Uncle Sam has sort of appointed himself the new Khalifa of the Muslim world.

The West has used its gold and guns to dominate the world. In the words of Huntington himself: "Through the UN and IMF and other international economic institutions (and now the WTO) the West promotes its economic interests and imposes on other nations the economic policies it thinks appropriate. The West in effect is using international institutions, military power and economic resources to run the world in ways that will maintain

Western predominance, protect Western interests and promote Western political and economic values."

And so you get unilateral US 301-Super, 301-Special sanctions. You get its GATT negotiator Carla Hills to say she will "pry open developing country markets with a crow-bar". You get the U.S. Secretary of State Madeleine Albright to say she doesn't care if five lac Iraqi children died as a result of American sanctions. And you get Kissinger to say that USA will not let India and China be friends under any circumstances.

Instead of righting these wrongs, the West is lecturing Asia on Democracy, Secularism, Human Rights and what not. Every country, every civilization, has its own view of these matters. And the West has no business to add social insult to economic injury. As Nixon noted in 1994: "Today's Chinese economic power makes U.S. lectures about human rights imprudent, within a decade irrelevant, and two decades hence, laughable." And so inspite of the over-powering attraction of USA, there is also much allergy to it. No wonder Huntington has noted: "At least two thirds of the World's people—Chinese, Russians, Arabs, Indians, Muslims and Africans—see the U.S. as the single great external threat to their societies. They do not regard America as a military threat but as a menace to their integrity, autonomy, prosperity and freedom of action" (vide 'Foreign Affairs, March-April, 1999). Clinton also recently wisely reminded the self-righteous America: "Here in the United States we were founded as a nation that practised slavery....This country looked the other way when a significant number of native Americans were dispossessed and killed to get their land or their mineral rights or because they were thought of as less than human beings. And we are still paying a price today."

Ms. Wendey, U.S. Ambassador in Pakistan has decided to fast during the month of Ramzan, like any Muslim. It is a good idea, a nice way of saying, "Let's be friends." But personal gestures cannot right global wrongs. Abiding world peace is not possible without a New World Order based on Justice.

The issue is not clash of civilizations; the issue very much is clash of vital interests.

□

Politicians and the Stars

Even Alexander, Napoleon and Reagan consulted astrologers.

President Ronald Reagan's erstwhile Chief of Staff, Donald Reagan, has revealed in his memoirs, *For the Record; From Wall street to Washington*, that the President and his wife Nancy are astrology buffs. Mrs. Reagan, says Regan, would often rule out important Presidential appearances and meetings on the ground that "the timing was not right". (This sounds very much like *Rahu Kaalam* when everything—including courts—come to a standstill in Tamil Nadu!) The White House has not denied the report; it said Mrs. Reagan "will continue to talk to her (astrologer Joan Quigley). She feels there's nothing wrong in talking to her". The spokesman even confirmed that the President "approved of it", that is of astrological consultation. The only White House objection is that the former aide had faulted not Mr. Reagan, but Mrs. Reagan, and that too on American 'Mother's Day'.

While kings and commoners may sympathise with the Reagans, over the unchivalrous aspect of the revelation, they can only be amazed and amused that the US President should have been programmed by astrologers. Some apologists for the White House have argued that Mrs. Reagan started consulting astrologers only after an attempt on Reagan's life on March 30, 1981—that is, for security reasons. But facts indicate otherwise. In his 1965 autobiography, *Where's the Rest Of Me*? Reagan wrote that astrologer Carroll Righter was "one of our good friends" and that "every morning Nancy and I turn to see what he has to say about people of our respective birth sign". (Reagan's sign is Aquarius.)

The more serious Americans are appalled that the head of the world's most powerful and advanced country should be consulting the stars for his daily engagements. But US humorists are having a field day over a 'star-war'-ring President turning out a star-gazing President. Chuckles Art Buchwald: "This country is blessed to have a Presidency and first Lady who believe in astrology. Where would we be if we had nobody to depend on but the CIA?"

However, it would seem that millions of Americans do believe in astrology. A recent survey showed that as many as 15% of them read astrological predictions every day; and more than half of them "decide to do or not do something because your astrological signs for that day are favourable or unfavourable."

It is of course ridiculous to be guided by the stars. And yet it would seem that astrology is not all baloney. In ancient and even medieval times, all princes—Hindu, Muslim, Christian—consulted the stars before they went to war. When Tipu was told the 'Sun' was against him, he had a golden sun made and he strapped it to his back!

Believe it or not but Josephine, wife of Napoleon, used to regularly visit Mademoiselle Lenormand, astrologer. Every time Napoleon would rebuke her for doing so. But after some time he would ask her what she had said. And when Josephine told him that she had predicted brilliant victories for him, he would break out in a broad smile—thus kind of okaying her future visits to her astrologer.

I once asked Shri B.V. Raman of *The Astrological Magazine*, how the stars could possibly affect man. And I still remember his reply. He said: "If the sun and the moon can generate ocean tides, why can't they influence small little creatures like men?" I must say he had a point.

We in India have always consulted the stars—and we continue to do so. Motilal Nehru used to show Jawaharlal's horoscope to Pandits. Many *pujas* used to be held for the health of Jawaharlal.

Indira also had many astrologers around her. India's hour of Independence—midnight of August 15, 1947—itself was settled in consultation with astrologers.

When C. Rajagopalachari was a young boy, a neighbour announced that astrologers had predicted that his son would become a big officer. At this, C.R.'s father could not contain what the astrologers had told him about his own son, namely that he will be 'king'. And C.R. became Governor-General of India!

During the Emergency in (Rohtak) Jail, I heard the experience of four leaders with astrologers. Ashok Mehta used to have a mangled thumb. I once asked him how it happened and he related: "The father of your Pandit (Vasant, who was a BJP leader of Bombay and a Ph.D. in astrology), a well-known astrologer, was a neighbour of ours. Once he told us that I should not move out of Bombay or do any driving on a particular day. I didn't care—and I even didn't remember. And then I casually left for Nasik by car on the forbidden day. On the way I had an accident and this thumb is a memento of that occasion. It was only when I got back to Bombay that we remembered what the astrologer friend had said."

Piloo Mody once related that when he was a child, astrologers had predicted that he will build many houses. "We thought I will become a great big landlord, living on rents. All that happened is that I became an architect, building houses for other people."

And then Jagannath Rao Joshi, then BJS M.P., had his own experience. "It was early forties and I was working in Military Accounts in Pune. Once I went home and my family was looking for a suitable match for me. And then an astrologer came and said, 'he will not marry, he will not maintain his family, but he himself will always be well looked after.' At that time the prediction seemed ridiculous. I was doing a job and sending money home and we were considering marriage proposals. But soon it became a fact. I resigned my job, became an RSS *Pracharak* and never married. My financial assistance to the family came to an end but, as an RSS *Pracharak*, my lodging and board were taken care of for life!"

At the time of the 1984 Lok Sabha elections, at a time when Vajpayee's re-election was taken for granted, astrologer after

astrologer said that his stars were adverse and that he will lose. They even added that if he did win, his adverse stars may take away his life. Fortunately, Atalji only lost the election!

Bhairon Singh Shekhawat had something even more interesting to tell. Astrologers had predicted a serious accident for him in the days to come. For days he did not stir out. When, however, a senior BJP leader was in town to address a public meeting, he cautiously moved out. With his weakness for *paan*, he stopped at a shop on the footpath to buy one. A tonga coming in speed, lost control, came over the footpath and shattered his leg. So many bones were fractured that the leg would have needed to be cut—had it not been that of Bhairon Singh who, as the top leader of Rajasthan, got the best medical attention at the earliest.

Only a few months before the Emergency, Dr. Vasant Pandit predicted that Mrs. Gandhi would soon impose an 'artificial emergency', throw thousands into jail, lose power and eventually die an 'unnatural death' (The Motherland, Jan. 26, 1975)!

And of course I have always wondered at Cheiro's predictions. He had told Miss Mary Leiter of USA that she would marry in royalty—and she married Curzon, and became Vicereine of India! Cheiro's other forecast in his *World Predictions*, published in 1927, was remarkable. He said that Hindu-Muslim violence would lead to the Partition of India. Later, he said, the two parts would re-unite.

Even more remarkable was his prediction in 1927 that the then Prince of Wales would not become king, that his brother would become king, whose stars would cause a World War. The elder Prince renounced (temporarily Edward VIII) the crown to marry a divorcee, Miss Simpson in 1937. Younger brother became George VI. World War came in 1939.

While there is no question of being slave to the stars—be they though, in the words of George Meredith, "the brains of heaven"—there is a case for an objective assessment of reputed astrologers and their predictions over the ages. For it is possible in the words of Hamlet, that

There are more things in heaven and earth, Horatio,
Than are dreamt of in your philosophy. □

APPENDIX

Salutation to Dr. Hedgewar!

Malkani's response to Dr. Hedgewar Pragya Samman, presented to him in Kolkata on April 18, 1999.

I must say I am overwhelmed by the Dr. Hedgewar Pragya Samman conferred on me for the year 1999. There cannot be a greater honour for a *Swayamsevak* than this Dr. Hedgewar Award. I did not have the good fortune of Dr. Saheb's *Darshan*. I was introduced to RSS a few weeks after he passed away in 1940. But I must say that his was a truly remarkable personality. Here was a man who did not have the advantage of wealth or ancestry. He did not have the support of Church or State. There was no press publicity, no apron-strings of an international movement. Actually all these forces were ranged against him. And yet he achieved almost the impossible—the vibrant revival of a sleepy Hindu Rashtra. And he did all this with nothing more than purity of heart, clarity of thought and sheer strength of will.

I feel fulfilled in having joined the RSS and become a small brick in the *Rashtra Mandir*. But how did I come to join the RSS?

My eldest brother, Prof. N.R. Malkani of revered memory, had resigned from the Bihar Education Service and joined Gandhiji in 1920. He repeatedly asked me to go to the *Shakha* and I started doing so. On January 26, 1942, I first went to the Congress meeting for the Independence Day pledge and then went to the *Shakha*, a little late. When the *Mukhya Shikshak* asked me why I was late and I told him the reason, he smiled a disapproving smile.

I went and told my Congressman brother: “Dada, you asked me to joint Sangha but RSS seems to be opposed to Congress.” Dada calmly replied: “I know that. But I find that Gandhiji does not appeal to educated youth. The RSS does. It will teach you how to live and, if necessary, how to die.” That was my rite of passage into the Sangh.

Although there was no occasion to lay down my life, I guess I did learn to live meaningfully enough. Way back in 1944, revered Baba Saheb Apte had introduced me in the Mumbai *Karyalaya* as: *Phaar Changla mulga aahay*. The fact that after fifty-five years of ups and down and trials and tribulations the *Mulga* remains *Changla*, is good enough proof that Sangh has taught me and many thousands of others—to live meaningfully. We are like those *ghunghroos* which do their duty wherever they are placed—be it in Press or platform, in Parliament or on TV. This honour is not an honour to an individual. It is a symbolic honour to all those *Swayamsevaks* who have lived and laboured for the sacred cause.

In 1925 when the RSS was founded, the challenge was dual: there was foreign rule and internal dissidence. Today the British are gone but the many weeds of casteism and communalism, Westernism and proselytism, planted by them, continue to flourish in various shapes and forms. But meanwhile a third and even more sinister threat has emerged on the scene. It is Market Fundamentalism. In the booming name of ‘globalisation’, efforts are afoot to penetrate the economy, erode the sovereignty and subvert the culture of nations. Some powerful countries and their MNCs are busy taking over the world. The old imperialism levied tribute; the new imperialism lends money on interest. Carla Hills, US Representative at the UN, threatened to “pry open developing country markets with a crow-bar.” However, the West must understand that the world is not for sale.

Samuel P. Huntington, that Prophet of Doom, has predicted 'Clash of Civilizations', but even he has had the honesty to admit that "Through the IMF and other international economic institutions, the West promotes its economic interests and imposes on other nations the economic policies it thinks appropriate. The West, in effect, is using international institutions, military power and economic resources to run the world in a way that will maintain Western predominance, protect Western interests and promote Western political and economic values."

Here is a serious bid for global imperialism. Such a dispensation will not only be unfair to Afro-Asia, it will cut at the Judeo-Christian-Hellenic roots of Western civilization itself. For by allowing profit motive to penetrate even cultural and moral fields of activity, global capitalism is debasing, demoralising and destroying society.

By preferring profits to employment, and by replacing Man by Money, it is finishing off Family and destroying Society as we know it. Even George Soros, himself the high priest of international finance, sees that "Market Fundamentalism is today a greater threat to open society than any totalitarian ideology." He fears that the developing world will rise in revolt against this new imperialism. And he predicts "the imminent disintegration of the global capitalist system."

Unless the West sees reason and stops throwing its economic, political, military and media weight around, it will soon find itself confronted by the Rest of the World. It will then be the West versus the Rest.

In this situation the spirit of *Swadeshi* will take centrestage in country after self-respecting country.

We in this country have a rich tradition of *Swadeshi*—Swadeshism not only of goods and services but of ideas and values.

No wonder Andre Malraux, the finest product of 20th century Europe, said: "There is no country like India" and "Gita is the Bible for the real revolution." And he told Nehru as early as the Thirties: "India does not belong to you, Mr. Nehru, though you say so; it belongs to me. India is the World's Holy Grail....Keep

India from duality. Let the great Shankaracharya guide India."

This was Greek to Nehru. But it evokes an immediate and powerful response in the Indian mind. As Ameury Riencourt noted in his *The Soul of India*: "Indian masses will only give their heart-felt allegiance to that party and ideology that appears to be a true emanation, more or less modernised no doubt, of some aspect or other of timeless Hinduism." It was "Gandhism yesterday" and it can only be "redoubtable RSS" tomorrow.

Under the leadership of BJP and the inspiration of RSS, India has gone nuclear, tried to build bridges with Pakistan and opted for *Swadeshi*, in the pursuit of its Manifest Destiny. The seed planted by Dr. Hedgewar has grown into a mighty tree. We have achieved much; but much more needs to be done. And there is no doubt that we will do it. For it is the call of the soul and the demand of the times. We will overcome. *Satyameva Jayate*!

□

Index

H

I

J

N

O

P

Q

R

U

V

W

Z

□□□